THE
IRISH CHRISTMAS BOOK

D0002075

REF   FORM 125 M

LITERATURE & LANGUAGE DIVISION

The Chicago Public Library

Received _____

765

THE IRISH CHRISTMAS BOOK

Edited by

John Killen

THE
BLACKSTAFF
PRESS

REF
8836.5
C48
I7
1985

First published in 1985
by The Blackstaff Press
3 Galway Park, Dundonald, Belfast BT16 0AN, Northern Ireland
and
51 Washington Street, Dover, New Hampshire 03820 USA
with the assistance of
The Arts Council of Northern Ireland

© This collection, Blackstaff Press, 1985
© Introduction, John Killen, 1985
All rights reserved

Printed in Northern Ireland
by The Universities Press Limited

British Library Cataloguing in Publication Data

The Irish Christmas book.
1. Christmas — Literary collections 2. English
literature — Irish authors
I. Killen, John
820.8'033   PR1111.C53

Library of Congress Cataloging-in-Publication Data

The Irish Christmas book.
Includes index.
1. Christmas — Literary collections. 2. English —
Literature — Irish authors.   I. Killen, John, 1954-
PR8836.5.C48I7   1985   820.8'33   85–22945

ISBN 0 85640 345 8

582 96728

CONTENTS

FOREWORD

It is said that we can best understand a country and its culture through its literature. In the case of the Irish Christmas the maxim certainly holds true; for nearly every major Irish writer (and a plethora of minor ones) has referred to the subject at some time or other. They have based novels, short stories, plays, poems and songs on the institution of Christmas, or set their action around the time of Christmas. Diarists of various eras have recorded the manner in which they spent their Christmas; folklorists have explained the origin and nature of our traditional customs; and annalists have set down those historic events which occurred in Ireland at this time of year.

Between the introduction of Christianity in the fifth century and the arrival of Elizabeth's military adventurers in the sixteenth, references to Christmas in Ireland are scant: but since the Elizabethan campaigns against 'the mere Irish' and the subsequent 'civilisation' of the country we are presented with a body of literature from which we can cull enlightening and entertaining information on the Irish Christmas. The *Annals of the Kingdom of Ireland* by the Four Masters tell us of the escape and the subsequent recapture of Red Hugh O'Donnell at Christmas time 1590 and of his second (successful) escape at Christmas two years later. From the manuscript account of Sir Josiah Bodley we learn how Christmas was kept in the barony of Lecale in County Down at the beginning of the seventeenth century, and from the writings of Sir Jonah Barrington we see how the 'gentry' passed a most memorable Christmas towards the end of the eighteenth century. The revelry of the nineteenth-century Irish peasant, his fondness for strong drink and his tendency towards bouts of violence are vividly treated by Mrs S.C. Hall and William Carleton, while writers like Cecil Frances Alexander and George Bernard Shaw respond to the season in vastly differing styles.

In the twentieth century the cheery security of the family Christmas as depicted by Elizabeth Hamilton is contrasted with the fragile facade of respectability in Frank O'Connor's account. James Joyce records how good food and politics did not mix at the Christmas table and Brendan Behan describes Christmas on remand in an English jail. Coming closer to the present, Benedict Kiely, Brendan Kennelly, Bernard MacLaverty, Seamus Heaney and Maeve Binchy all have their stories to tell.

Here then is a pot pourri of Irish Christmas celebrations; here the character of a people, their devotions and their superstitions, their shrewdness and their generosity, their riches and their poverty are laid before us. And, according to the talent and perceptiveness of the writer, we are informed, charmed, amused, saddened, enlightened or uplifted.

John Killen, 1985

CHRISTMAS EVE

Ruth and Celia Duffin

A cup of milk
And a wheaten-cake,
And a spark of fire
For the Travellers' sake.

A door on the latch,
A light in the pane,
Lest the Travellers pass
In the wind and rain.

For food and fire
And candlelight
The Travellers' blessing
On us this night.

Escape, 1929

THE CHRISTMAS RHYMERS

Lynn Doyle

There is a small white scar just on the crown of my head, now almost effaced by time. I wish it were not quite so faint. I received the wound many Christmases ago at the hands of no less a personage than Saint George. If you had met him the night he did the deed you would not have recognised him. He would appear to you in the shape of a sturdily-built youth of about fourteen. His body would be shrouded in a ragged white shirt, clearly the cast-off of an older and larger man, and girt about the waist with a rope of straw. The lower portion of his legs would be bound with straw-rope also. On his head instead of a halo there would be a top hat many sizes too large, tilted back to prevent his being completely engulfed, and wreathed with parti-coloured ribbon. Your natural curiosity to behold the countenance of a saint would be frustrated by a pasteboard vizard of horrific lineaments. On the whole you would have been in doubt whether you were looking at a saint at all, and if you had known as much about him as I did you would have been quite certain about it.

But do not suspect me of bearing malice. Saint George and I have shaken hands long ago, and are friends of, alas! how many years' standing. When we meet we forget the war and talk long of old times and pleasant memories. Not the least pleasant were the nights when he and I went Christmas-rhyming together, enacting the fragments, however debased, of a drama in which the original cast may have been Druids, and helping to keep alive a little longer the embers of an expiring tradition.

The members of our little company come back to me one by one. Some are alive, though changed; and others being dead are changeless. Little Tom Torrens still lives, and has married a wife twice as big as himself, and begotten sons and daughters at least half-a-score. It was for this quality of hardiness, even then apparent in him, that we chose him as our prologue, who must first spring from the sheltering darkness into the lighted kitchen where we found our stage, and foreshadow our mystery. His voice was, like himself, small; but it was shrill and clear enough, and he made a brave prologue:

Room, room, brave and gallant boys, come give us room to rhyme,
We come to show activity about these Christmas times,
Active youth and active age, the like was never acted on the stage,
And if you don't believe what I say enter in St George and he'll clear
  the way.

It was only last week that I heard young Tom – the latest of Old Tom's family except the twins – declaim the lines to an admiring kitchen-full of his relatives. He did it with a good deal of spirit and vigour, too; and his voice – it came to him from his mother's side of the house – is deeper than old Tom's was at his age; but though I didn't care to say so, I thought he wasn't a patch on what his father used to be.

I will not tell you what Saint George's name was in private life. Saint George has made money and bought land, and cuts some figure in the country. He is an elder of his Kirk these twenty years, and though he likes to talk with me in private about his Christmas Rhyming days, and some other small follies of his youth, I don't think he would like his family to know about them.

Robbie McKillop was our Oliver Cromwell. Peace be with him – he is dust these many years; but he was weak in the part. My cousin Barbara, despite her sex, was worth a dozen of him; but happening to catch sight of herself one night in an unexpected looking-glass was so alarmed by her own false-face with its portentous nose that she fell into hysterics, and threw up the part just as she was letter-perfect; so we had to fall back upon Robbie.

Our 'Doctor' was one Dick Semple, now also with the shades. His presence caused some scandal among the parents of our troupe; for his birth was esteemed humbler than became the company; but the demands of art prevailed. The 'Doctor' was our comic part, and Dick was inimitable in it.

Chubby little Mary Grant as befitted the future mistress of a gaunt three-storied farmhouse, plied the broom of Little Devil Doit as lustily as could be desired; but I marvel now at our sense of the fitness of things when we cast Winnie B — for Beelzebub. Surely a gentler spirit was never wronged by such a part, or a milder, sweeter countenance obscured by pasteboard wickedness. But she was tall and slim of shape, and cut a gallant figure in a red silk blouse, and a pair of her mother's long stockings, and scarlet trunks, with her skirts stuffed inside in the cause of propriety. If the real Prince of Darkness was abroad any of those murky nights, and we sometimes suspected it, he must have gnashed his teeth to see purity and innocence go by in his image. It was for Winnie's sweet sake I suffered by Saint George's sword. The fleeting touch of two cold lips on mine has left a more abiding wound than that it recompensed.

For weeks before Christmas my cousin Joseph's corn-loft was the scene of much sewing and snipping, and desperate contrivances of ribbons and patches not always lawfully acquired. No fragment of bright material was secure to our elders in the month of December. My aunt long deplored a remnant of green satin she lost one winter, and never knew it went to grace Saint Patrick's helm. Our ill-gotten finery never stayed with us. However glorious we went forth any Christmas,

the following one found us once more naked and predatory. For masks we sponged on my cousin Joseph, and never in vain. Each Christmas he unbuttoned his pockets he swore it was for the last time; but we knew cousin Joseph better than that.

It was always a very compact little band that travelled the roads on performing nights. In our pretended characters we felt ourselves more obnoxious than usual to the Powers of Darkness. It was safe enough to presume on the benevolence of Saint Patrick and Saint George towards our travesty of them; but then we had Beelzebub and Devil Doit among us, and never felt sure how the originals might take it. And though we carried a lantern we seldom dared to display the light. For one thing it was necessary to approach our victims' houses unperceived. But in addition to that, the appearance of a grotesquely-painted mask thrown up suddenly against the darkness is trying to nerves already a little on the strain. Dick Semple once paused unknown to us, to tie his bootlace, and when our lantern was flashed on him as he came running after, we took to our heels and ran a quarter of a mile. Even grown-ups found our false faces too much for them. Many a farmhouse door was barred early on our account for weeks before Christmas, not without reason. It was said that John Dorrian's first-born came untimely into the world through his mother's looking up from her seat by the kitchen hearth to behold the door 'with dreadful faces thronged'. There is a mark on her offspring's cheek to this day that every old woman in the country declare is the counterpart of Oliver Cromwell's nose. It is true that her doctor derided any connection between the two happenings; and I incline to believe him; but it cannot be denied that our irruptions some-times were the cause of more alarm than mirth. I myself saw Peter James Dolan sit down in a crock of cream well ripe for churning, at the entrance of prologue; and though cousin Joseph knew Peter James too well to believe he sacrificed the balance of the cream, he indemnified him for the irreparable ruin of his market-day trousers. I had a good set-off against the liability, having suffered damage in the same region through the action of Peter James's agent, an Irish terrier; for Peter James in his wrath had carried out an oft-repeated threat to 'put the dog on us'; but I was

4

too bashful to disclose it at the time, and let my cousin pay.

It was a matter of some strategy to gain an entrance to many houses. When after cautious raising of a latch we found a door barred we fell back on guile. Little Tom Torrens was our Sinon on these occasions. Knocking boldly on the door he tuned his piping voice to a pathetic key, and sobbed out some concocted tale of disaster. He had tripped over a stone and cut his knees on the road and required first-aid; or had fallen in a drain on his way home across the fields and needed drying; or he had been going to Jervis's shop for a loaf, and had dropped his sixpence, and could they let him have a blink of light, for if the sixpence were lost he would be beaten when he went home. No Greek that ever entered the Wooden Horse was wilier than little Tom. The tragedy in his voice would have melted rocks, let alone the heart of a farmer's wife with boys of her own. All this time we stood in a bunch at his elbow, breathless, creeping closer and closer with each sign of relenting within, ready to thrust in our sticks the instant a line of light along the door-post showed that the citadel was breached. Then with a headlong rush the door was flung back, and we poured tumultuously into the kitchen, not seldom over the prostrate body of the sentinel; and faithless Tom, bounding into the middle of the kitchen, broke into 'Room, room!' with all the shrillness of triumph. But having once gained an entrance we were never cast into outer darkness again until our play was played out. Perhaps no one was greatly deceived by our wiles.

In most farmhouses, indeed, we were received with pleasure. The floor was cleared of chairs to enlarge our stage. The grown-ups perched on tables to enjoy the show, with the elder boys and girls kneeling behind and peering over their shoulders; and sleepy children were brought rosy-faced and yawning from their beds, very often to return thither shrieking. In general, the mothers among our audience witnessed the show from 'the room' door, half-strangled by the arms of a clutching youngster, with one or two of the less terrified peering from the folds of her skirts, herself laughing and soothing in alternate breaths, and patting the affrighted one with comfortable hand. In such a house we ate and drank plenteously, and put money in our purse.

Yet strangely enough it is not our triumphs I recall most clearly. Far more vividly I remember the darkness, and the lashing rain, and the distant soughing wind, and tossing branches against pale rifts in the tattered clouds; or on our rare hard nights, the crackling rut-pools, and frosted hedges, and glittering rimy fields. I remember our night-alarms of moving sheep and belated cows, and the terror of angry dogs; and the Christmas Eve Devil Doit fell into the mill-race, and the night we saw the corpse-lights in the Quaggy bog.

An Ulster Childhood, 1921

Seajan·mac Cat maoil·del.

PIGS' FEET

W.R. Le Fanu

As I drove from Limerick one Christmas Eve an elderly woman with a small bundle in her hand ran after the car, holding on to the back of it. I got into coversation with her, and after some other talk I asked her what she had in her bundle.

'Tis some *cus-a-muck* (pigs' feet) I have, your honour, for Christmas.' After a pause she added, 'I got them for the price of a goose I sold in Limerick today.'

'Wouldn't the goose,' said I, 'have been better for dinner than the pigs' feet?'

'Av course it would, your honour, if we could ate her.'

'Why couldn't you?' said I.

'She was too ould and tough, your honour. I'm married twenty-five years ago last Shrove, and she was an ould goose then; and I'd never have sold her, only she was stoppin' of layin' by rason of her ould age.' She then began to laugh heartily, and said, 'It's what I'm laughing at, your honour, thinking of them that bought her, how they'll be breakin' the back of their heads against the wall tomorrow, strivin' with their teeth to pull the mate off her ould bones!'

Seventy Years of Irish Life, 1928

WHILE SHEPHERDS WATCHED THEIR FLOCKS BY NIGHT

Nahum Tate [1652–1715]

While shepherds watched their flocks by night,
All seated on the ground,
The angel of the Lord came down,
And glory shone around.

'Fear not,' said he, for mighty dread
Had seized their troubled mind;
'Glad tidings of great joy I bring
To you and all mankind.

'To you, in David's town, this day
Is born of David's line,
The Saviour, who is Christ the Lord,
And this shall be the sign:

'The heavenly babe you there shall find
To human view displayed,
All meanly wrapped in swaddling bands,
And in a manger laid.'

Thus spake the seraph; and forthwith
Appeared a shining throng
Of angels, praising God, who thus
Addressed their joyful song:

'All glory be to God on high,
And to the earth be peace;
Good will henceforth from Heaven to men
Begin and never cease.'

Oxford Book of Irish Verse, 1958

THE SEASON OF LIGHT

Eamon Kelly

As well as pattern day there is one other religious observance of long ago worth recalling. I'm thinking of Christmas. No word of a lie but it was something to write home about when I was small. Oh! the way we looked forward to twilight on Christmas Eve, for when darkness fell it was Christmas Night, the greatest night of all the year. We youngsters would be up with the crack of dawn that morning to have the house ready for the night.

Berry holly would have to be cut and brought in to deck out the windows, the top of the dresser, the back of the settle and the clevvy. We'd bring in ivy too and put a sprig of laurel behind the pictures, above the lintel of the door and around the fireplace. But we wouldn't overdo it, or if we did my mother would make us cut it down a bit, reminding us that she'd like to feel that she was in her own house for Christmas, and not in the middle of a wood!

Well, the transformation we could bring about in the kitchen with all that greenery! But we weren't finished yet. The Christmas candles had to be prepared; these were of white tallow as thick as the handle of a spade and nearly as tall. In some houses they'd scoop out a hole in a turnip and put the candle sitting into it. A big crock we'd use. We'd put the candle standing into that and pack it around with sand. If you hadn't sand, bran or pollard would do.

When the candle was firm in position we'd spike sprigs of holly or laurel into the sand about the candle, and we had coloured paper too to put around the outside of the crock to take the bare look off it. With that same coloured paper, the girls in the family, if they were anyway handy, could make paper flowers to decorate the holly. Then what would cap it all, was a length of young ivy and spiral it up around the candle – it looked lovely! That done, we would go through the same manoeuvre until there was a candle in a crock for every window in the house.

Then we'd be praying for night to fall, for you couldn't see the right effect until the candles were lit. That honour would fall to the youngest in the house. My father would lift him up saying: 'In the name of the Father and of the Son. . .' and when the child had blessed himself, he would put the lighting spill to the candle, and from that candle the other candles would be lit, and we'd be half daft with excitement, enjoying the great blaze of light, and running from the rooms to the kitchen and out into the yard to see what the effect was like from the outside. When we'd get tired of looking at the candles in our own windows, we'd turn and try to name the neighbours' houses as the bunches of lights came on, two windows here and three windows there, across the dark country-

8

side and away up to the foot of the hills. And as sure as anything someone'd be late and we'd rush into my mother saying:

'Faith, then there's no light on yet in Rosacrew!'

'Go on ye're knees!' my mother would say. The time she'd pick for the Rosary, just as the salt ling was ready and the white onion sauce and the potatoes steaming over the fire. But I suppose there'd be no religion in the world only for the women. The Rosary in our house didn't end at five decades. Not at all. After the Hail Holy Queen my mother would branch into the Trimmings:

> Come Holy Ghost send down those beams,
> Which sweetly flow in silent streams.

She'd pray for everyone in sickness and in need: the poor souls and the sinful soul that was at that very moment trembling before the Judgement seat above. She'd pray for the sailor on the seas: 'Protect him from the tempest, Oh Lord, and bring them safely home'. And the lone traveller on the highway and of course our emigrants and, last of all, the members of her own family:

> God bless and save us all
> St Patrick, Bridget and Colmcille
> Guard each wall.
> May the Queen of heaven
> And the angels bright
> Keep us and our house
> From all harm this night!

Our knees'd be aching as we got up off the floor, and it would take my father a while to get the prayer arch out of his back. Well, we wouldn't be sitting down to the supper when my mother'd bless herself again, a preliminary to grace before meals, and you could hardly blame my father for losing his patience.

'Is it in a monastery we are?' he'd say. 'Haven't we done enough praying for one night?'

After the supper there was Christmas cake for anyone with a sweet tooth. My father'd never look at that. His eye'd be on the big earthenware jar below the dresser, and it would be a great relief to him when my mother'd say to us:

'Go out there, one of ye, and tell the neighbouring men to come in for a while.'

It was the custom that night, *Nollaig Mhor*, big Christmas, for the men to visit each other's houses. The women were too busy to be bothered. They had their own night, *Nollaig na mBan*, small Christmas, for making tapes. In a while's time the men'd come, and at the first lag in the conversation my father'd take the cork off the jar and fill out a few cups

of porter. The men, by the way, not noticing what was going on, and then when they'd get the cups, all surprise they'd say:

'What's this? What's this for?'

'Go on take it,' my father'd say. 'It is Christmas night, neighbours, and more luck to us!'

Then the men's faces'd light up and lifting their cups they'd say:

'Happy Christmas, Ned. Happy Christmas, Hannie. Happy Christmas, everyone!'

'And the same to ye men,' my father would answer. 'May we all be alive again this time twelve months.'

And my mother, who was never very happy in the presence of strong drink, would direct her gaze in the direction of the Christmas candle and say:

'The grace of God to us all!'

After sampling the beverage one of the men putting out his lower lip to suck in any stray particles of froth that had lodged in his moustache would inquire:

'Where did you get this, Ned?'

'Carthy Dannehy's,' my father'd say.

'He always keeps a good drop, I'll say that for him.'

'*Sláinte*, Ned,' from all the men.

Sláinte chugat is cabhair
Dealbh go deo ná rabhair,
Is go bhfásfaidh gach ribín
Ar do cheann chomh fada le meigeal ghabhair.

The Rub of a Relic, 1978

10

THE GANDER

Padraig Ó Siochfhradha

We had a great time on Christmas Eve. Cait and myself got two big
turnips and cut them in half and made a hole in each of them to stand the
candles in. Then we stuck little branches of holly in them and Cait put a
frill of paper around them. They were lovely and we lit them long before
it was dark; but Mam put them out again.

That night, Mam put potatoes and fish on the table for us but neither
myself nor Cait ate a single bit, because we knew other things were on
the way. After a while, Mam took out the brack and cut it for us. Then
she made tea, and gave us an apple each.

When Mickileen's father passed by the door, Mam called him in and
gave him a drop from a bottle with three stars on it. She gave Dad a drop
too. Then she got a drink for herself from another bottle and they all
said, 'May we be alive this time next year,' whatever they meant by that.

Big-Betty and Mary-Andy came in next and Mam put a drop from the
yellow bottle into two glasses, added sugar and boiling water, and
stirred them with a spoon. At first I thought they wouldn't touch it.
Mary-Andy said.

'Oh! A drop of that would kill me!' But she downed it all the same, and
it didn't kill her either!

As the night wore on, a lot of young men came in and Mam gave them
their drinks out of the big jug. When I saw them all drinking, I got an
unmerciful longing for a drink, myself.

When Dad went out with Mickileen's father and Mam was talking to
the women over by the fire, I took a swig out of the jug. It's a wonder the
taste didn't kill me. I couldn't swallow it back, and was afraid to spit it
out on the floor. I ran out the door with my mouth full. Mam saw me.

'Where are you off to, now, Jimeen?' said she, but I couldn't say a
word. I opened the door and spat. She followed and saw me coughing
and wiping my mouth.

'Ha-ha,' said she, 'I wouldn't put it past you, you rascal. Weren't you
the nosey one?'

It was horrible stuff.

It was late when we went to bed that night, because Mam was getting
the goose ready for Christmas Day. She cleaned it out and washed it,
then stuffed it with boiled potatoes and onions and salt and pepper and
butter and loads of other things. She sewed it up with thread. Myself
and Cait were watching her.

On Christmas morning Cait and Mam went to first Mass. Myself and
Dad were left in charge. When Dad was milking the cows, I went to look
at the things in the cupboard. I took an apple and filled my pockets with

raisins. There was a piece of brack cut, so I took that too.

When I was closing the cupboard, a thought struck me – I took the yellow bottle and half-filled a cup. I tasted it, but boy, as bad as the black stuff was the night before, the yellow drink was seven times worse. It would burn the throat off you. I didn't know what to do with it. I called the dog and put the cup under his nose but he wouldn't look at it. All he did was sneeze.

Then I thought of another plan. I got a fistful of meal, wet it with the stuff from the bottle, and left it on a plate in the yard. The big gander gulped it all down. At first I didn't notice anything odd about him. Then he began to cackle. He stopped after a while, and started walking around with his head to one side. Round and round he went in a circle. Then he stopped, spread his legs apart and started shaking himself backwards and forwards. He'd make the cats laugh. Then he lay down and closed his eyes, for all the world like Old-Dermot when he dozes in the big chair by the fire.

Finally, he lay flat out on the ground, stretched his neck, spread his wings, and there wasn't a trace of life in him. It was as if he were dead. I was terrified that he'd die – and I didn't know what to do. I heard Dad coming in from the cowhouse and I ran inside. When Dad saw the gander he stopped and started talking to himself.

'Upon my word, but that fellow's really plastered,' he said. 'Jimeen,' he yelled.

I was sweeping the floor like mad. I came to the door.

'What did you do to the gander?' said Dad.

I stopped. I didn't like to hide the truth on Christmas morning, so I told Dad the story, in fits and starts. I could see he wasn't pleased.

'You'll pay for your tricks some day, my boy,' said he. 'And I suppose it was you finished off the cat, too, down in Poulalin?'

I thought I'd fall out of my standing. I didn't think a living soul knew about that. I felt sheepish then. I thought, of course, that Dad would tell Mam everything. I went to Mass and prayed all through it that God would keep me safe from all the trouble threatening me.

When I came home, Mam had the gander beside the fire, and he was recovering. She never found out what happened to him because, when Dad came home, she was trying to find out from him who'd come in that morning and got whiskey.

Dad was making a joke of the whole thing and wouldn't tell her. He threw me a look that left me feeling quite uneasy.

Still, Dad's all right.

Jimeen (translated by Patricia Eagan,
Peter Fallon and Ide Ni Laoghaire, 1984)

12

IN LIEU OF CAROLS

Frank Ormsby

Setting out in darkness this Christmas Eve
I find the countryside is brewing mist
In all its hollows. Out of it the wet
Lane unravels, hatches every yard
A tree, a fence, the dull outline of fields.
My way is to the shop to buy matches.

Beyond the hedge the black shapes of cattle,
Trampling mudholes, shadow me to the road.
I cannot see their smoky breath, but feel
Its warmth. If there be stars among the sights
The mist has hidden, good! Enough for now
To make my journey following cottage lights.

A Store of Candles, 1977

CHRISTMAS IN OLD DUBLIN 1

Annie M.P. Smithson

Nowadays, when we think of Christmas, we associate the festival with turkeys, plum pudding, mince pies and so on. This kind of festival was practically unknown to our ancestors, and we undoubtedly got these notions from England.

The English fashion of keeping Christmas has changed through the centuries. We know that in the Middle Ages it was kept with great pomp and pageantry; in Puritan times it was forbidden to keep the festival at all, for it was regarded as a 'popish' feast. After the Restoration we may suppose that Christmas was again popular, but later on it must have fallen upon evil days, for one of the titles bestowed upon Charles Dickens by his countrymen was 'the man who discovered Christmas'. And most certainly his books, especially his famous *Christmas Carol* and *Christmas Stories*, did an immense amount to revive the keeping of the festival of Christmas in England.

We got the idea of the plum pudding and mince pies from England; from that country also – by way of Germany, in the person of the Prince Consort – came the idea of the Christmas tree. I once spent a Christmas in the County of Donegal and found that plum pudding and mince pies were unknown amongst the people, and the children had never seen a Christmas tree.

One would like to visualise the first Christmas in Dublin after the introduction of Christianity. Was St Patrick there? We know that he visited Dublin in the year 448, but we have no records that I know of relating to the keeping of Christmas in that year. But there is one thing certain, and that is, that the Feast would not have been so material a thing as it often is in these modern days. It would have been a great religious festival above all else; feasting and drinking would have taken a secondary place. Indeed, so far as we can gather from our history and records, at no time were the Gaelic people great eaters, nor did they ever care for the pleasures of the table to the same extent as did the English.

We have proof of this fact when we come to the next Christmas I will mention. It is in the year of Our Lord 1171; Henry II has been excommunicated for his complicity in the murder of St Thomas à Becket, and has crossed to Ireland to spend his Christmas here. We are told that the Irish chieftains who were present at the royal feast were disgusted at the amount and quality of the food on the tables. They were particularly surprised to see the English eating the flesh of cranes, swans, and peacocks; they considered that such food as crane's flesh was not fit to eat. Henry caused to be built a great palace of wattlework, erected in the Irish fashion, and it stood where College Green is now. How strange to

look backward and to try to imagine what Dublin looked like on that Christmas night of 1171.

Readers of *Sketches of Old Dublin*, by A. Peter, will remember the account of Christmas in Dublin in the year 1458. The big event in those days seems to have been the performance of the religious dramas called Miracle Plays. The Lord Deputy at that time was the Earl of Ossory, and he received an invitation from the citizens of Dublin to be present at a new play on every day of that week. Those were the days of the powerful City Guilds and these plays were all enacted by members of those Guilds. The performance took place in Hoggen Green – College Green as we now call it.

It should not be hard to draw a picture in our minds of Hoggen Green as it was in that Christmas of 1458. A large stage was erected and the open space before it was filled with spectators. Of course there was lots of room – the neighbourhood being almost open country then. For the Deputy and his friends, no doubt, special seats were reserved, but we can see the citizens, rich and poor, all striving to get a good view of the actors. What was the weather like? And which of us today would stand for hours – the plays were very long – in the open air in December to witness a play? And yet I suppose it might really be much healthier for us than sitting in the vitiated atmosphere of our theatres and picture-houses. Anyway, these ancestors of ours were hardy folk, and probably never bothered about weather conditions unless they were extreme altogether. Let us hope for their sakes that it was dry and frosty by day, with stars overhead at night, when they crowded to Hoggen Green to stare open-eyed at the players.

The Shoemakers acted the story of their patron, St Crispin; the Bakers gave a comedy in which the goddess of Corn appeared; the Smiths represented Vulcan in all his power; to the Carpenters fell the honour of portraying the story of the Nativity. One cannot but be struck with the extraordinary manner in which heathen mythology and the truths of Christianity were mixed together in those old plays. The queerest play of all, to my mind, was that of Adam and Eve, which was enacted by – of all people, the Guild of Tailors! After these plays were finished, others, dealing with incidents in the life of Our Lord and His Apostles, were ordered to be staged, by command of the Prior of All Hallows. Surely the citizens of Dublin had their full of theatrical displays in that Christmas week of 1458.

Dublin Historical Record, 1943

CHRISTMAS

Cecil Frances Alexander

Once in royal David's city
Stood a lowly cattle shed,
Where a Mother laid her Baby
In a manger for His bed;
Mary was that Mother mild,
Jesus Christ her little child.

He came down to earth from Heaven
Who is God and Lord of all,
And His shelter was a stable,
And His cradle was a stall;
With the poor, and mean, and lowly,
Lived on earth our Saviour Holy.

And through all His wondrous Childhood,
He would honour and obey,
Love, and watch the lowly Maiden,
In whose gentle arms He lay;
Christian children all must be
Mild, obedient, good as He.

For He is our childhood's pattern,
Day by day like us He grew,
He was little, weak, and helpless,
Tears and smiles like us He knew
And He feeleth for our sadness,
And He shareth in our gladness.

And our eyes at last shall see Him,
Through His own redeeming love,
For that Child so dear and gentle
Is our Lord in Heav'n above;
And He leads His children on
To the place where He is gone.

Not in that poor lowly stable,
With the oxen standing by,
We shall see Him; but in Heaven,
Set at God's right hand on high;
When like stars His children crown'd
All in white shall wait around.   Amen.

Poems, 1896

16

CHRISTMAS IN KESH POLICE-BARRACKS

J. Anthony Gaughan

There are two places which few people would select for a Christmas holiday, one is the county jail and the other is a police-barracks. Of the two I would say that the county jail would be the more cheerful. In the barracks the bare white tables and deal forms provided the only furniture, while leather belts, batons, swords, and police caps took the place of pictures cn the walls. The library consisted of piles of Acts of Parliament which everybody detested, while the diary and patrol-book held a prominent place to remind one that duty was always calling, even at Christmas.

As in many other respects Kesh was the great exception. For a whole week before Christmas presents of geese and turkeys were arriving and Christmas greetings came from far and wide, from friends whom we had met on our long cycling tours during the summer and from tourists whom we had entertained during their trips around Kesh. In the lock-up we had four cases of stout and several bottles of whiskey, which we received from our publican-friends. Although stout was then only twopence per pint and whiskey fivepence per glass, we accepted the presents for what they were, genuine tokens of friendship and not in any way calculated to be bribes.

On Christmas Eve we had just taken the usual precautionary cycle spins around the district to make sure that all was well and were settling down to enjoy our Christmas when the peace of the district was temporarily disturbed by an old man, named Horan, who lived alone about a half-mile from the barracks. Returning from Kelly's pub he was well under the influence of drink and halted at the barracks gate. Here he shouted abuse at the top of his voice, and throwing off his coat, challenged the police to come out. At first we ignored him but this only encouraged him to shout louder. Eventually he attracted the attention of the curate who lived across the road. Reluctantly it was decided that action would have to be taken, but how? We could not arrest him as the lock-up was filled with valuable goods. The sergeant, as usual, came to the rescue. Walsh and myself were instructed to escort Horan home, get him to bed and remain with him until he was asleep. This was rather distasteful work on Christmas Eve night but anything was preferable to upsetting our improvised canteen.

Leaving Horan at home was not as simple as we had expected, as he resisted violently. This we overcame by borrowing an ass-and-cart from the local publican and into the cart went Horan, Walsh and myself. A few people returning home after eleven o'clock on Christmas Eve night enjoyed the spectacle of two of their policemen in the ass-and-cart, one driving and the other holding down Horan, who was shouting at the top of his voice. Horan refused point blank to go to bed and we had to sit in the kitchen for at least two hours until he eventually went to sleep on the chair. Having taken off his boots we got him into bed and for some time we watched him while he slept peacefully, dreaming, perhaps, of his four fine sons who were far away across the Atlantic. Walsh had very thoughtfully taken a drop of whiskey in his pocket and he left this on a chair beside the bed with a note 'From the RIC with the compliments of the season. Call at the barracks first thing in the morning.' Early on Christmas morning poor old Horan called expecting to get a summons for 'drunk and disorderly behaviour'. Instead he got another glass of whiskey and a good breakfast of turkey and ham with an invitation to call back for his dinner which he did.

During the whole Christmas week all duty was suspended in so far as doing the ordinary patrols were concerned. Each day, of course, we took a spin round on the bicycles and made the usual discreet inquiries and 'found all regular'. The unwritten law in the RIC, the sergeant told me on one occasion, was to 'keep sober and shaved and keep the diary and patrol-book up to date and you can't be sacked'. This law was strictly kept at Kesh during Christmas and did not in the least interfere with the dances and card-playing parties which were held during the Christmas period.

Memoirs of Constable Jeremiah Mee, RIC, 1975

POLITICS AT CHRISTMAS

James Joyce

A great fire, banked high and red, flamed in the grate and under the ivytwined branches of the chandelier the Christmas table was spread. They had come home a little late and still dinner was not ready: but it would be ready in a jiffy his mother had said. They were waiting for the door to open and for the servants to come in, holding the big dishes covered with their heavy metal covers.

All were waiting: uncle Charles, who sat far away in the shadow of the window, Dante and Mr Casey, who sat in the easychairs at either side of the hearth, Stephen, seated on a chair between them, his feet resting on the toasted boss. Mr Dedalus looked at himself in the pierglass above the mantelpiece, waxed out his moustache ends and then, parting his coat tails, stood with his back to the glowing fire: and still from time to time he withdrew a hand from his coat tail to wax out one of his moustache ends. Mr Casey leaned his head to one side and, smiling, tapped the gland of his neck with his fingers. And Stephen smiled too for he knew now that it was not true that Mr Casey had a purse of silver in his throat. He smiled to think how the silvery noise which Mr Casey used to make had deceived him. And when he had tried to open Mr Casey's hand to see if the purse of silver was hidden there he had seen that the fingers could not be straightened out: and Mr Casey had told him that he had got those three cramped fingers making a birthday present for Queen Victoria.

Mr Casey tapped the gland of his neck and smiled at Stephen with sleepy eyes: and Mr Dedalus said to him:

– Yes, Well now, that's all right. O, we had a good walk, hadn't we, John? Yes. . . I wonder if there's any likelihood of dinner this evening. Yes. . . O, well now, we got a good breath of ozone round the Head today. Ay, beded.

He turned to Dante and said:

– You didn't stir out at all, Mrs Riordan?

Dante frowned and said shortly:

– No.

Mr Dedalus dropped his coat tails and went over to the sideboard. He brought forth a great stone jar of whisky from the locker and filled the decanter slowly, bending now and then to see how much he had poured in. Then replacing the jar in the locker he poured a little of the whisky into two glasses, added a little water and came back with them to the fireplace.

– A thimbleful, John, he said, just to whet your appetite.

Mr Casey took the glass, drank, and placed it near him on the

19

mantelpiece. Then he said:

– Well, I can't help thinking of our friend Christopher manu-facturing. . .

He broke into a fit of laughter and coughing and added:

– . . . manufacturing that champagne for those fellows.

Mr Dedalus laughed loudly.

– Is it Christy? he said. There's more cunning in one of those warts on his bald head than in a pack of jack foxes.

He inclined his head, closed his eyes, and, licking his lips profusely, began to speak with the voice of the hotel keeper.

– And he has such a soft mouth when he's speaking to you, don't you know. He's very moist and watery about the dewlaps, God bless him.

Mr Casey was still struggling through his fit of coughing and laughter. Stephen, seeing and hearing the hotel keeper through his father's face and voice, laughed.

Mr Dedalus put up his eyeglass and, staring down at him, said quietly and kindly:

– What are you laughing at, you little puppy, you?

The servants entered and placed the dishes on the table. Mrs Dedalus followed and the places were arranged.

– Sit over, she said.

Mr Dedalus went to the end of the table and said:

– Now, Mrs Riordan, sit over. John, sit you down, my hearty.

He looked round to where uncle Charles sat and said:

– Now then, sir, there's a bird here waiting for you.

When all had taken their seats he laid his hand on the cover and then said quickly, withdrawing it:

– Now, Stephen.

Stephen stood up in his place to say the grace before meals:

Bless us, O Lord, and these Thy gifts which through Thy bounty we are about to receive through Christ our Lord. Amen.

All blessed themselves and Mr Dedalus with a sigh of pleasure lifted from the dish the heavy cover pearled around the edge with glistening drops.

Stephen looked at the plump turkey which had lain, trussed and skewered, on the kitchen table. He knew that his father had paid a guinea for it in Dunn's of D'Olier Street and that the man had prodded it often at the breastbone to show how good it was: and he remembered the man's voice when he had said:

– Take that one, sir. That's the real Ally Daly.

Why did Mr Barrett in Clongowes call his pandybat a turkey? But Clongowes was far away: and the warm heavy smell of turkey and ham and celery rose from the plates and dishes and the great fire was banked

high and red in the grate and the green ivy and red holly made you feel so happy and when dinner was ended the big plum pudding would be carried in, studded with peeled almonds and sprigs of holly, with bluish fire running around it and a little green flag flying from the top.

It was his first Christmas dinner and he thought of his little brothers and sisters who were waiting in the nursery, as he had often waited, till the pudding came. The deep low collar and the Eton jacket made him feel queer and oldish: and that morning when his mother had brought him down to the parlour, dressed for mass, his father had cried. That was because he was thinking of his own father. And uncle Charles had said so too.

Mr Dedalus covered the dish and began to eat hungrily. Then he said:

– Poor old Christy, he's nearly lopsided now with roguery.

– Simon, said Mrs Dedalus, you haven't given Mrs Riordan any sauce.

Mr Dedalus seized the sauceboat.

– Haven't I? he cried. Mrs Riordan, pity the poor blind.

Dante covered her plate with her hands and said:

– No, thanks.

Mr Dedalus turned to uncle Charles.

– How are you off, sir?

– Right as the mail, Simon.

– You, John?

– I'm all right. Go on yourself.

– Mary? Here, Stephen, here's something to make your hair curl.

He poured sauce freely over Stephen's plate and set the boat again on the table. Then he asked uncle Charles was it tender. Uncle Charles could not speak because his mouth was full; but he nodded that it was.

– That was a good answer our friend made to the canon. What? said Mr Dedalus.

– I didn't think he had that much in him, said Mr Casey.

– *I'll pay your dues, father, when you cease turning the house of God into a pollingbooth.*

– A nice answer, said Dante, for any man calling himself a catholic to give to his priest.

– They have only themselves to blame, said Mr Dedalus suavely. If they took a fool's advice they would confine their attention to religion.

— It is religion, Dante said. They are doing their duty in warning the people.

— We go to the house of God, Mr Casey said, in all humility to pray to our Maker and not to hear election addresses.

— It is religion, Dante said again. They are right. They must direct their flocks.

— And preach politics from the altar, is it? asked Mr Dedalus.

— Certainly, said Dante. It is a question of public morality. A priest would not be a priest if he did not tell his flock what is right and what is wrong.

Mrs Dedalus laid down her knife and fork, saying:

— For pity sake and for pity sake let us have no political discussion on this day of all days in the year.

— Quite right, ma'am, said uncle Charles. Now, Simon, that's quite enough now. Not another word now.

— Yes, yes, said Mr Dedalus quickly.

He uncovered the dish boldly and said:

— Now then, who's for more turkey?

Nobody answered. Dante said:

— Nice language for any catholic to use!

— Mrs Riordan, I appeal to you, said Mrs Dedalus, to let the matter drop now.

Dante turned on her and said:

— And am I to sit here and listen to the pastors of my church being flouted?

— Nobody is saying a word against them, said Mr Dedalus, so long as they don't meddle in politics.

— The bishops and priests of Ireland have spoken, said Dante, and they must be obeyed.

— Let them leave politics alone, said Mr Casey, or the people may leave their church alone.

— You hear? said Dante, turning to Mrs Dedalus.

— Mr Casey! Simon! said Mrs Dedalus, let it end now.

— Too bad! Too bad! said uncle Charles.

— What? cried Mr Dedalus. Were we to desert him at the bidding of the English people?

— He was no longer worthy to lead, said Dante. He was a public sinner.

— We are all sinners and black sinners, said Mr Casey coldly.

— *Woe be to the man by whom the scandal cometh!* said Mrs Riordan. *It would be better for him that a millstone were tied about his neck and that he were cast into the depths of the sea rather than that he should scandalise one of these, my least little ones.* That is the language of the Holy Ghost.

— And very bad language if you ask me, said Mr Dedalus coolly.

— Simon! Simon! said uncle Charles. The boy.

— Yes, yes, said Mr Dedalus. I meant about the. . . I was thinking about the bad language of that railway porter. Well now, that's all right. Here, Stephen, show me your plate, old chap. Eat away now. Here.

He heaped up the food on Stephen's plate and served uncle Charles and Mr Casey to large pieces of turkey and splashes of sauce. Mrs Dedalus was eating little and Dante sat with her hands in her lap. She was red in the face. Mr Dedalus rooted with the carvers at the end of the dish and said:

— There's a tasty bit here we call the pope's nose. If any lady or gentleman. . .

He held a piece of fowl up on the prong of the carving-fork. Nobody spoke. He put it on his own plate, saying:

— Well, you can't say but you were asked. I think I had better eat it myself because I'm not well in my health lately.

He winked at Stephen and, replacing the dishcover, began to eat again.

There was a silence while he ate. Then he said:

— Well now, the day kept up fine after all. There were plenty of strangers down too.

Nobody spoke. He said again:

— I think there were more strangers down than last Christmas.

He looked round at the others whose faces were bent towards their plates and, receiving no reply, waited for a moment and said bitterly:

— Well, my Christmas dinner has been spoiled anyhow.

— There could be neither luck nor grace, Dante said, in a house where there is no respect for the pastors of the church.

Mr Dedalus threw his knife and fork noisily on his plate.

— Respect! he said. Is it for Billy with the lip or for the tub of guts up in Armagh? Respect!

— Princes of the church, said Mr Casey with slow scorn.

— Lord Leitrim's coachman, yes, said Mr Dedalus.

— They are the Lord's anointed, Dante said. They are an honour to their country.

— Tub of guts, said Mr Dedalus coarsely. He has a handsome face, mind you, in repose. You should see that fellow lapping up his bacon and cabbage of a cold winter's day. O Johnny!

He twisted his features into a grimace of heavy bestiality and made a lapping noise with his lips.

— Really, Simon, you should not speak that way before Stephen. It's not right.

— O, he'll remember all this when he grows up, said Dante hotly – the language he heard against God and religion and priests in his own home.

– Let him remember too, cried Mr Casey to her from across the table, the language with which the priests and the priests' pawns broke Parnell's heart and hounded him into his grave. Let him remember that too when he grows up.

Portrait of the Artist as a Young Man, 1916

"Who is it, mater—Bernard Shaw?"

NO MUSIC AT CHRISTMAS

George Bernard Shaw

20 December 1893

Like all intelligent people, I greatly dislike Christmas. It revolts me to see a whole nation refrain from music for weeks together in order that every man may rifle his neighbor's pockets under cover of a ghastly general pretence of festivity. It is really an atrocious institution, this Christmas. We must be gluttonous because it is Christmas. We must be drunken because it is Christmas. We must be insincerely generous; we must buy things that nobody wants, and give them to people we don't like; we must go to absurd entertainments that make even our little children satirical; we must writhe under venal officiousness from legions of free-booters, all because it is Christmas – that is, because the mass of the population, including the all-powerful middle-class tradesman, depends on a week of licence and brigandage, waste and intemperance, to clear off its outstanding liabilities at the end of the year. As for me, I shall fly from it all tomorrow or next day to some remote spot miles from a shop, where nothing worse can befall me than a serenade from a few peasants, or some equally harmless survival of medieval mummery, shyly proffered, not advertised, moderate in its expectations, and soon over.

Music in London, 1890–94, 1932

'BOYCOTTED' AT CHRISTMASTIDE

Bernard H. Becker

Kilfinane, Co. Limerick, Christmas Eve

The fox-terrier sits blinking on the hearth-rug in the pretty drawing-room as nightfall approaches, and a servant appears with a message that a woman has come with a big cake from Mrs O'Blank, a sympathising neighbour. There is no mistake about the size and condition of the cake; it is a yard and a quarter in circumference; it has a shining holiday face, like that of the fabled pigs who ran about ready roasted, covered with delicately-browned 'crackling', perfumed with sage and onions, and carrying huge bowls of apple-sauce in their mouths. As the pigs cried, 'Come and eat me,' so does the cake appeal, but in more subtle manner, to the instincts and nostrils of all present. It has that pleasant scent with it peculiar to newly-baked plumcake. Huge plums, which have worked their way perseveringly to the surface, wink invitingly, and, above all, the cake is hot, gloriously hot, besides having with it a delicate zest of contraband acquired by being smuggled on to the premises under Biddy McCarthy's shawl.

Biddy has watched the moment when the 'boys' on the watch – scowling ruffians by the same token – had gone in quest of tea or more potent refreshment, and has slipped from the avenue which runs past the house instead of up to it, by the lodge gate and up to the door in that spirit-like fashion peculiar to this part of Ireland. When they wish to do so, the people appear to spring out of the ground. Two minutes before the monotony of existence is broken by a fight there will not be a soul to be seen, but no sooner is it discovered that some unlucky wight is in present receipt of a 'big bating' than hundreds appear on the spot, and struggle for a 'vacancy', like the lame piper who howled for the same at the 'murthering' of a bailiff.

This ghost-like faculty, however, has served us right well, for I need not speculate upon what would have happened to Mrs McCarthy (whose real name is not given for obvious reasons) if she had been discovered carrying a huge cake to a house under ban. She would not have been injured bodily; no soul in Kilfinane would have touched the cake, much less have eaten the hateful food made and baked and attempted to be carried to the stronghold of the 'tyrant'; but it would have gone ill with the brave little woman nevertheless. Her husband would have been compelled to seek elsewhere for a livelihood, for neither farmer nor tradesman would dare to employ either him or her. Her elder children would have been pointed at as they went to school, and sent to Coventry while there; and she would have been refused milk for the younger ones. Not a potato nor a pound of meal nor an egg could she have bought all through the hamlet; and if people at a distance had sold her anything, they would have been intercepted and compelled to take it back again. The carriers would not have delivered to or taken parcels from her.

Disturbed Ireland, 1881

CHRISTMAS AT COOLE

Lady Gregory

26 December. The adjournment of the Dail gives one breathing time and hope! And Christmas has passed peacefully. I miss the workhouse children now it is closed, after so many years. Robert used to come with me to give them toys and the old men their tobacco, and last year I had Richard and Anne with me. Our Christmas tree here, Guy and Olive staying in the house, Bagots, officers, MFH, etc. Today the wrenboys came, knowing but few lines about the wren. Some sang the Soldiers Song, and two of the groups gave a song about Kevin Barry.

Lady Gregory's Journals, Vol. 1, 1921

RED HUGH'S ESCAPE, CHRISTMAS 1590

The Four Masters

Hugh Roe O'Donnell had [now] been in captivity in Dublin for the space of three years and three months. It was [a cause of] great distress of mind to him to be thus imprisoned; yet it was not for his own sake [that he grieved], but for the sake of his country, his land, his friends, and kinsmen, who were in bondage throughout Ireland. He was constantly revolving in his mind the manner in which he might make his escape. This was not an easy matter for him, for he was confined in a closely-secured apartment every night in the castle until sunrise the next day. This castle was surrounded by a wide and very deep ditch, full of water, across which was a wooden bridge, directly opposite the door of the fortress; and within and without the door were stationed a stern party of Englishmen, ·closely guarding it, so that none might pass in or out without examination. There is, however, no guard whose vigilance may not some time or other be baffled. At the very end of winter, as Hugh and a party of his companions were together, in the beginning of the night, before they were put into the close cells in which they used to be every night, they took with them a very long rope to a window which was near them, and by means of the rope they let themselves down, and alighted upon the bridge that was outside the door of the fortress. There was a thick iron chain fastened to this door, by which one closed it when required; through this chain they drove a strong handful of a piece of timber, [and thus fastened the door on the outside], so that they could not be immediately pursued from the fortress. There was a youth of Hugh's faithful people [outside] awaiting their escape, and he met them on coming out, with two well-tempered swords concealed under his garments; these he gave into the hand of Hugh, who presented one of them to a certain renowned warrior of Leinster, Art Kavanagh by name, who was a champion in battle, and a commander in conflict.

As for the guards, they did not perceive the escape for some time; but when they took notice of it they advanced immediately to the door of the castle, for they thought that they should instantly catch them. Upon coming to the gate, they could not open it; whereupon they called over to them those who happened to be in the houses on the other side of the street, opposite the door [of the castle]. When these came at the call, and took the piece of timber out of the chain, and threw open the door for the people in the castle, who [then] set out, with a great number of the citizens, in pursuit of the youths who had escaped from them; but this was fruitless, for they [the fugitives] had passed beyond the walls of the city before they were missed, for the gates of the regal city had been wide open at the time; and they pursued their way across the face of the

28

mountain which lay before them, namely, *Sliabh Ruadh*, being afraid to venture at all upon the public road, and never halted in their course until after a fatiguing journey and travelling, they had crossed the red mountain aforesaid. When, weary and fatigued, they entered a thick wood which lay in their way, where they remained until morning. They then attempted to depart, for they did not deem it safe to remain in the wood, from fear of being pursued; but Hugh was not able to keep pace with his companions, for his white-skinned [and] thin feet had been pierced by the furze of the mountain, for his shoes had fallen off, their seams having been loosened by the wet, which they did not till then perceive. It was great grief to his companions that they could not bring him any further; and so they bade him farewell, and left him their blessing.

He sent his servant to a certain gentleman of the noble tribes of the province of Leinster, who lived in a castle in the neighbourhood, to know whether he could afford them shelter or protection. His name was Felim O'Toole, and he was previously a friend to Hugh, as he thought, for he had gone to visit him on one occasion in his prison in Dublin, when they formed a mutual friendship with each other. The messenger proceeded to the place where Felim was, and stated to him the embassy on which he came. Felim was glad at his arrival, and promised that he would do all the good he could for Hugh; but his friends and kindred did not allow him to conceal him, from fear of the English government.

These learned that he was in the wood, as we have said, and they (i.e. the people who had heard that he was in the wood) went in search of him, and dispersed with their troops to track him. When it was clear to Felim that he [Hugh] would be discovered, he and his kinsmen resolved to seize upon him themselves, and bring him back to the Council in the city. This was accordingly done. When he [Hugh] arrived in Dublin, the Council were rejoiced at his return to them; for they made nothing or light of all the other prisoners and hostages that had escaped from them. He was again put into the same prison, and iron fetters were put upon him as tightly as possible; and they watched and guarded him as well as they could. His escape, thus attempted, and his recapture, became known throughout the land of Ireland, at which [tidings] a great gloom came over the Irish people.

Annals of the Kingdom of Ireland, 1632–36
  (translated by John O'Donovan, 1851)

CHRISTMAS DAY IS COME

Luke Wadding [1588–1657]

Christmas Day is come; let's all prepare for mirth,
Which fills the heav'ns and earth at this amazing birth.
Through both the joyous angels in strife and hurry fly,
With glory and hosannas; 'All Holy' do they cry,
In heaven the Church triumphant adores with all her choirs,
The militant on earth with humble faith admires.

But why should we rejoice? Should we not rather mourn
To see the Hope of Nations thus in a stable born?
Where are His crown and sceptre, where is His throne sublime,
Where is His train majestic that should the stars outshine?
Is there not sumptuous palace nor any inn at all
To lodge His heav'nly mother but in a filthy stall?

Oxford Book of Irish Verse, 1958

CHRISTMAS ALMS

Douglas Hyde

In the old time there was a married couple living near Cauher-na-mart, in the County Mayo. They had seven of a family, but God sent them worldly means, and they wanted for nothing but the love of God.

The man was a pious and generous person, and was good to the poor, but the wife was a hard miser without mercy, who would not give alms to man or stranger, and after refusing the poor man she used not to be satisfied with that, but she used to give him abuse also. If a person able to do work were to come looking for alms from her, she would say, 'Unless you were a lazy vagabond you would not be here now looking for alms and bothering my head with your talk', but if an old man or an old woman who could do no work would come to her, it is what she would say to them that they ought to be dead long before that.

One Christmas night there was frost and snow on the ground. There was a good fire in Patrick Kerwan's house – that was the man's name – and the table was laid. Patrick, his wife, and his family were siting down at the table, and they ready to go in face of a good supper when they heard a knock at the door. Up rose the wife and opened it. There was a poor man outside, and she asked him what he was looking for.

'I'm looking for alms in the honour of Jesus Christ, who was born on this festival night, and who died in the cross of passion for the human race.'

'Begone, you lazy guzzler,' she said, 'if you were one half as good at working as you are at saying your prayers, you would not be looking for alms to-night, nor troubling honest people,' and with that she struck the door to, in the face of the poor man, and sat down again at the table.

Patrick heard a bit of the talk she give the poor man, and he asked who was at the door.

'A lazy good-for-nothing, that was looking for alms,' she said, 'and if it wasn't that it was a lazy vagabond that was in it, he could not come looking for alms from people who are earning their share of food hardly, but he would sooner be saying his old prayers than working for meat.'

Patrick rose; 'bad was the thing you did,' said he, 'to refuse anyone for a morsel of meat, and especially to refuse him on Christmas night. Isn't it God that sent us everything that we have; there is more on this table than will be eaten to-night, how do you know whether we shall be alive to-morrow?'

'Sit down,' says she, 'and don't be making a fool of yourself, we want no sermons.'

'May God change your heart,' says Patrick, and with that he got the full of his two hands of bread and food, and out with him, following the

31

poor man, going on the track of his feet in the snow as quick as he could, till he came up with him. He handed him the food then, and told him he was sorry for his wife's refusing him, 'but,' says he, 'I'm sure there was anger on her.'

'Thank you for your food,' said the poor man. He handed the food back again to him, and said, '(there), you have your food and your thanks, (both). I am an angel from heaven who was sent to your wife in the form of a poor man, to ask alms of her in the honour of Jesus Christ, who was born this night, and who suffered the passion of the Cross for the human race. She was not satisfied with refusing me, but she abused me also. You shall receive a great reward for your alms, but as for your wife she shall not be long until she is standing in the presence of Jesus Christ to give Him an account of the way in which she spent her life on this world.'

The angel departed, and Patrick returned home. He sat down, but he could neither eat nor drink.

'What's on you?' says the wife, 'did that stroller do anything to you?'

'My grief! It was no stroller was in it, but an angel from heaven who was sent to you in the shape of a man to ask alms of you, in honour of Jesus Christ, and you were not satisfied with refusing him, but you must abuse him with bad names. Now, your life on this world is not long, and in the name of God, I beseech you, make a good use of it.'

'Hold your tongue,' she said, 'I think that you saw a ghost, or that you lost your senses, and may God never relieve you, nor anyone else who would leave a good fire, and a good supper, running out in the snow after a lazy rap; but the devil a much sense was in you ever.'

'If you don't take my advice, you'll repent when you'll be too late,' said Patrick; but it was no use for him to be talking.

When Little Christmas (New Year's Day) came, the woman was not able to get dinner ready; she was deaf and blind. On the Twelfth Night she was not able to leave her bed, but she was raving and crying, 'give them alms, alms, alms, give them everything in the house in the name of Jesus Christ'.

She remained for a while like that, between the death and the life, and she without sense. The priest came often, but he could do nothing with her. The seventh day the priest came to her, and he brought the last oil to anoint her with.

The candles were lit, but they were quenched upon the spot. They tried to light them again, but all the coals that were in the county Mayo would not light them. Then he thought to put the oil on her without a candle, but on the spot the place was filled with a great smoke, and it was little but the priest was smothered. Patrick came to the door of the room, but he could go no further. He could hear the woman crying, 'a drink, a drink, in the name of Christ!'

She remained like this for two days, and she alive, and they used to

32

hear her from time to time crying out 'a drink, a drink,' but they could not go near her.

Word was sent for the Bishop O'Duffy, and he came at last, and two old friars along with him. He was carrying a cross in his right hand. When they got near Patrick's house, there came down on them with one swoop a multitude of kites, and it was little but they plucked the eyes out of the three.

They came then to Patrick's door and they lit the candles. The bishop opened a book and said to the friars, 'When I shall begin reading the prayers do ye give the responses.' Then he said, 'Depart O Christian soul –'

'She is not a Christian soul,' said a voice, but they saw no one.

The Bishop began again, 'Depart O Christian soul out of this world, in the name of the all-powerful Father who created you –'. Before he could say more there came great thunder and lightning. They were deafened with the thunder: the house was filled with smoke. The lightning struck the gable of the house and threw it down. The deluge came down so that the people thought it was the end of the world that was in it.

The Bishop and the two friars began at their prayers again. 'O Lord according to the abundance of Thy mercy, look mercifully upon her,' said the Bishop. 'Amen,' said the friars. There came a little calm and the Bishop went over to the bed. Poor Patrick came to the other side of the bed, and it was not long till the woman opened her mouth and there came a host of dardeels* out of it. Patrick let a screech and ran for fire to put on them. When he came back the woman was dead, and the dardeels gone.

The Bishop said prayers over her, and then he himself went away and the two friars, and Patrick went out to get women to wash the corpse, but when he came back the body was not to be found either up or down. There was a purse round its neck, and the purse went with the body, and there is no account of either of them from that out.

*The Dardeel, or Dharadeel, is a chafer or beetle with a cocked tail, the most loathsome insect known to the Irish peasant. It was he betrayed Our Lord in the Irish Legend. He is always burnt in Connacht. They call him a 'crocodile' in English.

The Religious Songs of Connacht, 1906

SINGING AWAY TO THEMSELVES
ABOUT THEMSELVES

Harry Barton

'In the fourteenth century,' said Mr Mooney, 'I used to spend Christmas near a fountain called St Agnes' Fountain. This place was underneath a mountain and right up against a forest fence. The mountain was Drumnagortihacket Mountain and the fence had been put there by the Northern Ireland Forestry Department of that time. About three miles away – or, as we used to put it in those days, a good league hence – there was a castle. This castle belonged to a king called Wenceslas, who was supposed to be a good king – though, in my opinion,' said Mr Mooney, 'he wasn't in the same class as our Kings Billy and James.'

'I thought that Wenceslas was King of Bohemia.'

'He was,' said Mr Mooney.

'What was he doing with a castle in County Derry, then?'

'He was an absentee landlord,' he said. 'Like all kings. James and William were the same. They never actually lived here. They only came here to fight their battles. Wenceslas, however, was in the habit of coming to his Ulster castle for a week or two around Christmas time; and when he was in residence I used to make a point of trudging sorrowfully through the snow under the castle windows, gathering winter fuel in the moonlight.'

'But why would you want to do that?'

'There was a fuel crisis every winter in those days. The turf-cutters of Ballyrashnatamnacloghan always went on strike when it snowed. They asked for rugged duty money. They claimed that the snow was so deep and crisp and even that they couldn't get at the turf beneath.'

'And why would you go gathering fuel around the castle? I would have thought that would have been the last place.'

'What I wanted was the King's attention,' said Mr Mooney, 'and in the end, one Boxing Day towards the close of the fourteenth century, I heard him call for his page and I knew that he had seen me. He was at his

34

window, thirty feet up, and his crown gleamed in the moonlight. He did not so much call for the page as sing for him in his deep voice:

Hither page and stand by me
If thou knowest it telling
Yonder peasant who is he
Where and what his dwelling?

'There was a pause and then I heard the page's treble voice reply:

Sire, he lives a good league hence
Underneath the mountain,
Right against the forest fence
By St Agnes' Fountain.

'Proper little know-all that page,' said Mr Mooney. 'Knew everything about everyone.'

'I don't see why you would want to attract the attention of King Wenceslas at all.'

'This was Christmas time,' said Mr Mooney, 'I wanted flesh, wine and pine logs; and for a time it looked as though I was going to get all three. The King now sang:

Bring me flesh and bring me wine,
Bring me pine logs hither.
Thou and I shall see him dine
When we bear them thither.'

'You're a rich leprechaun,' I said. 'There was no need for you to go conning that poor king into parting with his pine logs and his goodies. You could have made him a present of a huge Yule Log of solid fairy gold, and your fairy bank manager wouldn't have blinked.'

'There was a ninety per cent FGPL embargo in force at the time.'

'FGPL?'

'The Fairy Gold Producing Leprechauns had reduced supplies to a trickle,' said Mr Mooney. 'They thought they were being funny. They were driving round Ireland in tiny medieval Cadillacs making unmentionable gestures with their fingers at everyone.

'I had to eat,' he said. 'Even a leprechaun has to eat.'

Yours Again, Mr Mooney, 1974

WHEN MARY THE MOTHER KISSED THE CHILD

Charles G.D. Roberts

When Mary the Mother kissed the Child
And night on the wintry hills grew mild,
And the strange star swung from the courts of air
To serve at a manger with kings in prayer,
Then did the day of the simple kin
And the unregarded folk begin.

When Mary the Mother forgot the pain,
In the stable of rock began love's reign.
When that new light on their grave eyes broke
The oxen were glad and forgot their yoke;
And the huddled sheep in the far hill fold
Stirred in their sleep and felt no cold.

When Mary the Mother gave of her breast
To the poor inn's latest and lowliest guest –
The God born out of the woman's side –
The Babe of Heaven by Earth denied –
Then did the hurt ones cease to moan,
And the long-supplanted came to their own.

When Mary the Mother felt faint hands
Beat at her bosom with life's demands,
And nought to her were the kneeling kings,
The serving star and the half-seen wings.
Then was the little of earth made great,
And the man came back to the God's estate.

The Gael, December 1902

CHRISTMAS CUSTOMS IN CORK

Mr and Mrs S.C. Hall

For some weeks preceding Christmas, crowds of village boys may be seen peering into the hedges, in search of the 'tiny wren'; and when one is discovered, the whole assemble and give eager chase to, until they have killed, the little bird. In the hunt the utmost excitement prevails; shouting, screeching, and rushing; all sorts of missiles are flung at the puny mark; and, not unfrequently, they light upon the head of some less innocent being. From bush to bush, from hedge to hedge, is the wren pursued until bagged, with as much pride and pleasure as the cock of the woods by the more ambitious sportsman. The stranger is utterly at a loss to conceive the cause of this 'hubbub', or the motive for so much energy in pursuit of 'such small game'. On the anniversary of St Stephen (the 26th of December) the enigma is explained. Attached to a huge holly-bush, elevated on a pole, the bodies of several little wrens are borne about. This bush is an object of admiration in proportion to the number of dependent birds, and is carried through the streets in procession, by a troop of boys, among whom may be usually found 'children of a larger growth', shouting and roaring as they proceed along, and every now and then stopping before some popular house – such as that of Mr Olden, the 'distinguished inventor' of EVKEROGENION (a liquid soap) and half-a-dozen other delightful and useful things, to which he has given similar classical names – and their singing 'the wren boys' song, of the air which a professional friend, Mr Alexander D. Roche, has 'penned' down for us:–

To the words we have listened a score of times, and although we have found them often varied according to the wit or poetical capabilities of a leader of the party, and have frequently heard them drawled out to an apparently interminable length, the following specimen will probably satisfy our readers as to the merit of the composition:–

> The wran, the wran, the king of all birds,
> St. Stephen's day was cot in the furze;
> Although he is little, his family's grate –
> Put yer hand in yer pocket and give us a trate.
>   Sing holly, sing ivy – sing ivy, sing holly,
>   A drop just to drink it would drown melancholy.
> And if you dhraw it ov the best,
> I hope in heaven yer sowl will rest;
> But if you dhraw it ov the small,
> It won't agree wid'de wran boys at all.

Of course contributions are levied in many quarters, and the evening is, or rather was, occupied in drinking out the sum total of the day's collection.

The accompanying sketch, from the pencil of Mr Maclise, will describe better than language can do the singular ceremony, and the fantastic group by whom it is conducted. This is, we believe, the only Christmas gambol remaining in Ireland of the many, that in the middle ages were so numerous and so dangerous as to call for the interposition of the law, and the strong arm of magisterial authority. As to the origin of the whimsical but absurd and cruel custom, we have no data. A legend, however, is still current among the peasantry which may serve in some degree to elucidate it.

In a grand assembly of all the birds of the air, it was determined that the sovereignty of the feathered tribe should be conferred upon the one who would fly highest. The favourite in the betting-book was, of course, the eagle, who at once, and in full confidence of victory, commenced his flight towards the sun; when he had vastly distanced all competitors, he proclaimed with a mighty voice his monarchy over all things that had wings. Suddenly, however, the wren, who had secreted himself under the feathers of the eagle's crest, popped from his hiding-place, flew a few inches upwards, and chirped out as loudly as he could, 'Birds, look up and behold your king'.

There is also a tradition, that in 'ould ancient times', when the native Irish were about to catch their Danish enemies asleep, a wren perched upon the drum, and woke the slumbering sentinels just in time to save the whole army; in consequence of which, the little bird was proclaimed a traitor, outlawed, and his life declared forfeit wherever he was thenceforward encountered.

Another old custom prevails also to some extent. May eve, the last day of April, is called 'Nettlemas night', boys parade the streets with large bunches of nettles, stinging their playmates, and occasionally bestowing a sly touch upon strangers who come in their way. Young and merry maidens, too, not unfrequently avail themselves of the privilege to 'sting' their lovers; and the laughter in the street is often echoed in the drawing-room. These are the only customs peculiar to Cork, if we except that of 'the Christmas candle'. A tallow candle is formed, as in the annexed print, without question to commemorate 'the Trinity', it is lit at three ends on Christmas eve, and burned until midnight. It is then extinguished, and carefully preserved during the year as a protection against the visits of all evil spirits – except whiskey.

Ireland, Its Scenery, Character, etc., 1841/3

Seaʒan·mac Cacmaoil·del.

CHRISTMAS IN IRELAND LONG AGO

Denis A. McCarthy

At Christmas, Christmas in Ireland long ago,
The blazing log upon the hearth gave out a cheery glow,
And lit the kindly faces that I used to love and know,
At Christmas, Christmas in Ireland long ago!

At Christmas, Christmas in Ireland long ago,
The holly on the dresser crowned the dishes in a row,
The Christmas candle beaming threw the light across the snow,
At Christmas, Christmas in Ireland long ago!

At Christmas, Christmas in Ireland long ago,
Without the wind might bluster, and without the wind might blow,
Within was peace among us and the kind word to and fro,
At Christmas, Christmas in Ireland long ago.

At Christmas, Christmas in Ireland long ago,
I mind the merry music of the fiddle and the bow,
I mind a song we used to sing together soft and slow.
At Christmas, Christmas in Ireland long ago.

At Christmas, Christmas in Ireland long ago,
I mind a hand that led me through the darkness and the snow,
To see Our Saviour lying in a manger, rude and low,
At Christmas, Christmas, in Ireland long ago!

Ah, Christmas, Christmas, in Ireland long ago! –
Your memories are dearer still the older that I grow,
And harder 'tis to keep them back – the tears so fain to flow
For Christmas, Christmas, in Ireland long ago!

Green and Gold, 1920

WINTER WILDLIFE

Giraldus Cambrensis

WOLVES THAT WHELP IN DECEMBER

Wolves in Ireland generally have their young in December, either because of the extreme mildness of the climate, or rather as a symbol of the evils of treachery and plunder which here blossom before their season:

RAVENS AND OWLS THAT HAVE THEIR YOUNG ABOUT CHRISTMAS-TIME

About Christmas-time of the year when Lord John first left the island, ravens and owls in many parts of the country had their young. Perhaps they foretold the occurrence of some new and premature evil.

The History and Topography of Ireland, 1185

THE NATIVITY

C.S. Lewis

Among the oxen (like an ox I'm slow)
I see a glory in the stable grow
Which, with the ox's dullness might at length
Give me an ox's strength.

Among the asses (stubborn I as they)
I see my Saviour where I looked for hay;
So may my beastlike folly learn at least
The patience of a beast.

Among the sheep (I like a sheep have strayed)
I watch the manger where my Lord is laid;
Oh that my baa-ing nature would win thence
Some woolly innocence!

Poems, 1964

AONAĊ NA NODLAG

Anon

For the last few years the National Council have conferred a real benefit on us at Christmas by organising an Irish fair at the Rotunda, AONAĊ NA NODLAG. This fair is a place were every possible variety of Irish soul can have appropriate Christmas presents selected for it, all Irish manufactured, so that the fountain of cash flung up at this time of the year will fall back into an Irish basin. The organisers of the Irish fair cater indifferently for the body and the soul. The poetically inclined can buy Maunsell's poets, the artistically inclined will find upstairs a whole gallery of modern Irish art, the smoker can get Irish tobacco to put into an Irish pipe, the Dun Emer and Cuala industries have both stalls filled with their beautiful art work. We direct special attention to a calendar for 1911, printed at Cuala, with one of those magical drawings of Jack Yeats, which bring us back to life as an eternally new adventure. The belly will not lack for fulness if it seeks an Irish stuffing here in the fair; even the child can be solaced by Irish sweets. The maiden can be made fairer in the eyes of her beloved by being clad in Irish materials which can be bought here. The young man likewise after a visit to this place can get clothed and be in his right patriot mind. Whatsoever an Irish heart desires, from an Irish boot to stand on to an Irish hat to sit on him can be obtained. Here are stalls for everybody with everything they want. We were glad to see the stalls of the various firms were well patronised. The body of the Rotunda was filled very much as in former years by enterprising stallholders. The greatest improvement visible was in the art section, where the younger Irish artists had a display of real merit. We are obviously going to have a squad of young Irish artists to balance the troop of young Irish poets. We noticed specially some little paintings by Paul Henry, a new name to us, but a real artist, with a mastery over his materials and a feeling for colour and composition which should carry him far. We understand this artist will have a separate exhibition of his own later on in Dublin, which will be looked for with much interest. The brothers Morrow, a talented family who can between them write plays, stage manage them, and act in them, decorate houses, illustrate *Punch*, paint landscapes or figures with equal facility and power, have many good pictures here. Mrs Sinclair with her 'Windy Day' gives us the feeling she lives among mountains and large things. Miss Perrott's little painting of 'Dollymount' anybody would like to have on their walls. Miss Solomons gives us 'A Grey Day' with a silver lining to it which we liked very much. Jack Yeats has an overflow exhibition here of good sketches. Miss Gifford in her 'Bailey Lighthouse' has got something curiously like Conder mixed with something which is distinctively her own. This little sketch shows what a talent Miss Gifford has. Will she work? The elder Yeats is represented by pencil portraits, in which his supremacy is unquestioned. Nobody can use the difficult lead so well as he can. Mrs Marsh's 'Suffolk Farm' was pleasing in composition and colour. Mr Gerald Festus Kelly, who has gained a great reputation in England, sends three pictures, of which we like best the 'Archway in Cairo'. We have not space to do more than direct attention to some interesting work by Miss Hamilton, F. O'Donoghue, Count Markievicz, J.P. Campbell, and Miss Williams. Everybody interested in painting should go to see this show at the Aonac before it closes on Saturday, the 17th inst.

The Irish Homestead, 1910

TO THESE HIGH LANDS A STRANGER,
BY ANCIENT MEMORY DRAWN,
I GO TO FIND THE MANGER,
BY THE DIM ROADS OF DAWN.
O STARS THAT SANG HIS STORY
AND SAW MY KING PASS BY,
LEAN STILL IN LINGERING GLORY
AND LIGHT MY MORNING SKY.
                    SUSAN L. MITCHELL

CUALA PRESS
DUNDRUM

THE ESCAPE OF RED HUGH AND ART O'NEILL

The Four Masters

Hugh Roe, the son of Hugh, son of Manus O'Donnell, remained in Dublin, in prison and in chains, after his first escape to the winter of this year [1592]. One evening he and his companions, Henry and Art, the sons of O'Neill (John), before they had been brought into the refection house, took an advantage of the keepers, and knocked off their fetters. They afterwards went to the privy-house, having with them a very long rope, by the loops of which they let themselves down through the privy-house, until they reached the deep trench that was around the castle. They climbed the outer side, until they were on the margin of the trench. A certain faithful youth, who was in the habit of visiting them, and to whom they had communicated their secret, came to them at this time, and guided them. They then proceeded through the streets of the city, mixing with the people; and no one took more notice of them than of any one else, for they did not delay at that time to become acquainted with the people of the town; and the gates of the city were wide open. They afterwards proceeded by every intricate and difficult place, until they arrived upon the surface of the Red Mountain over which Hugh had passed in his former escape. The darkness of the night, and the hurry of their flight (from dread of pursuit), separated the eldest of them from the rest, namely, Henry O'Neill. Hugh was the greenest of them with respect to years, but not with respect to prowess. They were grieved at the separation of Henry from them; but, however, they proceeded onwards, their servant guiding them along. That night was snowing, so that it was not easy for them to walk, for they were without [sufficient] clothes or coverings, having left their outer garments behind them in the privy-house, through which they had escaped. Art was more exhausted by this rapid journey than Hugh, for he had been a long time in captivity, and had become very corpulent from long confinement in the prison. It was not so with Hugh; he had not yet passed the age of boyhood, and had not [yet] done growing and increasing at this period, and his pace and motion were quick and rapid. When he perceived Art had become feeble, and that his step was becoming inactive and slow, he requested him to place one arm upon his own shoulder, and the other upon that of the servant. In this manner they proceeded on their way, until they had crossed the Red Mountain, after which they were weary and fatigued, and unable to help Art on any further; and as they were not able to take him with them, they stopped to rest under the shelter of a high rocky precipice which lay before them. On halting here, they sent the servant to bring the news to Glenmalur, where dwelt Fiagh, the son of Hugh [O'Byrne], who was then at war with the

45

English. This is a secure and impregnable valley; and many prisoners who escaped from Dublin were wont to resort to that valley, for they considered themselves secure there, until they could return to their own country. When the servant came into the presence of Fiagh, he delivered his message, and how he had left the youths who had escaped from the city, and [stated] that they would not be overtaken alive unless he sent them relief instantly. Fiagh immediately ordered some of his servants of trust (those in whom he had most confidence) to go to them, taking with them a man to carry food, and another to carry ale and beer. This was accordingly done, and they arrived at the place where the men were. Alas! Unhappy and miserable was their condition on their arrival. Their bodies were covered over with white-bordered shrouds of hail stones freezing around them on every side, and their light clothes and fine-threated shirts too adhered to their skin; and their large shoes and leather thongs to their shins and feet; so that, covered as they were with the snow, it did not appear to the men who had arrived that they were human beings at all, for they found no life in their members, but just as if they were dead. They were raised by them from their bed, and they requested of them to take some of the meat and drink; but this they were not able to avail themselves of, for every drink they took they rejected again on the instant: so that Art at length died, and was buried in that place. As to Hugh, after some time, he retained the beer; and after drinking it, his energies were restored, except the use of his two feet, for they were dead members, without feeling, swollen and blistered by the frost and snow. The men carried him to the valley which we have mentioned, and he was placed in a sequestered house, in a solitary part of a dense wood, where he remained under cure until a messenger came privately from his brother-in-law, the Earl O'Neill, to inquire after him.

Annals of the Kingdom of Ireland, 1632–36
  (translated by John O'Donovan, 1851)

A CHRISTMAS CHILDHOOD

Patrick Kavanagh

I

One side of the potato-pits was white with frost –
How wonderful that was, how wonderful!
And when we put our ears to the paling-post
The music that came out was magical.

The light between the ricks of hay and straw
Was a hole in Heaven's gable. An apple tree
With its December-glinting fruit we saw –
O you, Eve, were the world that tempted me

To eat the knowledge that grew in clay
And death the germ within it! Now and then
I can remember something of the gay
Garden that was childhood's. Again

The tracks of cattle to a drinking-place,
A green stone lying sideways in a ditch
Or any common sight the transfigured face
Of a beauty that the world did not touch.

II

My father played the melodeon
Outside at our gate;
There were stars in the morning east
And they danced to his music.

Across the wild bogs his melodeon called
To Lennons and Callans.
As I pulled on my trousers in a hurry
I knew some strange thing had happened.

Outside the cow-house my mother
Made the music of milking;
The light of her stable-lamp was a star
And the frost of Bethlehem made it twinkle.

A water-hen screeched in the bog,
Mass-going feet
Crunched the wafer-ice on the pot-holes,
Somebody wistfully twisted the bellows wheel.

My child poet picked out the letters
On the grey stone,
In silver the wonder of a Christmas townland,
The winking glitter of a frosty dawn.

Cassiopeia was over
Cassidy's hanging hill,
I looked and three whin bushes rode across
The horizon – the Three Wise Kings.

An old man passing said:
'Can't he make it talk' –
The melodeon. I hid in the doorway
And tightened the belt of my box-pleated coat.

I nicked six nicks on the door-post
With my penknife's big blade –
There was a little one for cutting tobacco.
And I was six Christmases of age.

My father played the melodeon,
My mother milked the cows,
And I had a prayer like a white rose pinned
On the Virgin Mary's blouse.

Collected Poems, 1964

CHRISTMAS HOLIDAY

Benedict Kiely

She lived in Main Street. On Boxing Day Peter called to see her. The street before the shop was crowded, red-coated men on horses, red-coated women, men and women with ordinary dull clothes, a noisy pack of hounds, listless spectators. Katie, the maid, opened the door, the hall-door opening into a long passage separated from the shop by a thin partition. He followed Katie's corseted stiffness up the stairs into the living-room. Rita sat in a low chair near the window, bending forward slightly to look into the street.

'Katie,' she said, 'tell Daddy that Peter is here. Sit down, Peter.'

He sat near the fire, watching the room reflected in the heavy over-mantel: the solid, well-cushioned chairs fashionable forty years ago; the ornate grapes-and-flowers sideboard; the period portraits, figures in a dark centre against a white, empty background, women in great skirts; whiskered, stiff-collared men.

'Not interested in the harriers, Peter?'

'Not much.'

'Wouldn't blame you.'

She moved from the window, depositing the fruit-dish on a tiny inlaid table, came to sit facing him across the glow of the fire. She went on talking, hastily.

'The harrier people are a class. Or the remnants of a class. They've degenerated so much that the foxes left the country. If they rise a few hares now they consider their luck's in. They ride round fields too, looking for the gate.'

Peter smiled. He said: 'Poor Somerville and Ross.'

'Of course,' she said, 'this never was a great country for hunting. The farmers must have thought too much of their land. The Presbyterians were great men for barbed wire.'

Down in the street a horn blared. The dogs bayed. She said: 'John Peel, how are you!'

He watched her pale face taking a blush of heat from the glow of the fire. Loosened hair fell down dark on the shoulders of a white blouse. A dark skirt curved with her slim muscular body. She crossed her ankles, lazily stretching towards the heat, and for a moment he was conscious of something familiar displayed by the discarding of that self-protective hardness. He caught his breath, troubled, perplexed. The door opened and her father came into the room. A big, genial man in his late fifties. Fair hair had turned grey and thinned, leaving an abnormally wide expanse of forehead above a round, healthy face. There was loose good-nature in the cut of his great limbs. The compactness of body, the thrusting force of the spirit in his daughter came obviously from the dead mother. He swung forward a great hand.

'Welcome, Mister Quinn. And how did you over Christmas?'

'Very well indeed, Mr Keenan.'

'Quiet, I suppose.'

'That's a blessing nowadays.'

'Do you think will Hitler beat them?'

'Maybe.'

The big man went silent, staring into the fire, thinking of the weekly pension that came to him as a retired sergeant of the old Irish constabulary. The war would hit the cloth trade. Every shilling counted.

He said: 'I hope to God not.'

Rita, rising, passed round the fruit-dish. They munched, talking little.

Rita said: 'You'll eat something, Peter?'

'Not after a Christmas dinner.'

'You can have the leavings of ours. We live on scraps for the week after Christmas.'

'This war is bad,' said her father. 'Now, in the last war there was money to be made. Carneys made it in sawmills, Dohertys made it at coachbuilding and at the groceries. They own the town now.'

'That money won't pass the third generation,' said the girl. 'Look at Alec Carney drinking himself into paralysis.'

'But this war isn't the same. No money to be made except at smuggling. Decent men ruined that never knew a day's idleness.'

'It'll end sometime,' Peter said.

'You're young, Mister Quinn. You haven't lived to see two wars. I have. When the last war was on I talked the way you talk now. Then we lived through the troubled times: shooting and burning, the riots in Belfast, feared of our lives, not knowing under God which side was the worst.'

Rita chanted: 'A policeman's lot.'

'Then things settled an' we made our homes. We thought peace would last for ever.'

In the street again the horn blared and the hounds bayed. They heard the clatter of moving hooves, the shuffle of feet. She walked to the window.

'There's Carter the milkman. He rides with the hunt now. They say his horse stops at every door when they ride through the town.'

'Where's your brother?'

'Jack's down in the street watching the hunt. He left here to buy some new dance music in Jacksons, but the crowd held him.'

'You still run the school?'

'They have me deaf,' said the father. 'An' dead for want of sleep. Two nights a week blowing music and teaching the town how to dance.'

'HIS MASTER'S VOICE'

'It pays. Somebody else would do it if we didn't. Keenan's school of ballroom dancing. We teach Irish dancing now too. You should see the hall since we fixed it up. Painted in blue and gold.'

'I'd love to.'

She turned from the window, looked at the clock.

'We'd have time before dinner to look at it.'

'I'm not hungry.'

'Still, you'll eat something with us. For old time's sake.'

She was suddenly smiling, almost blushing, her eyes alive and bright, the hardness melting and vanishing. He watched her, feeling some powerful attraction, some longing, then reacting into alarm at his own unspoken accordance with her mood, her whim.

From the hallway at the bottom of the stairs a sidedoor opened on a cobbled yard. He followed her across the cobbles to the green door of the dancing-hall, set into a wall of whitewashed brick. There was a cold emptiness in the place; two grates with fires set, the dead white wood and black flameless coal intensifying the cold. Coloured-paper hangings drooped dead and lifeless from the roof, ringed the four windows that from their higher level overlooked walls and back gardens, the slow river fringed with ice, the long bridge of red metal.

'We have a dance to-night. You should come, Peter.'

She went up the steps to the platform used by the dance band. On a table she fingered at and opened a small portable gramophone.

'Wouldn't suit my cloth, Rita.'

'You could look on. You needn't dance.'

'Looking on isn't much fun.'

'Do you want fun?'

Her eyes and mouth were laughing, but in her voice there was an echo of mockery, of malice. He looked through a window over the walls and gardens, the river, the red bridge. The mockery maddened him, showed him how easily he could end it, showed him also that it would never end unless he said certain words: a sentence, a phrase, and mockery would end leaving only laughter in the eyes, rich laughter on the mouth. He couldn't say the words. They would end a vision, seen dimly by himself, distinctly by his mother. No mockery with her, only patience, conviction, endless hope.

The needle scraped on a worn record, a band played scrapily, male voices sang, a ball-bearing rattled in each voice: 'We're going to hang out our washing on the Siegfried Line.' She said: 'Davy wouldn't like it. It's a new one. You can quick-step to it.'

51

Davy. The name was reality, rock-bottom. He came away from the window, from the unreal dreams, the quicksands, the treachery of the twisting current that pulled and pulled. He said suddenly: 'Put that thing off, Rita. I don't want to dance.'

She laughed. 'Nobody asked you.'

The record played. She came slowly down the steps from the platform and stood by his side, her hand on his shoulder, lightly at first, then the fingers gripped and held as he made to move away.

'You don't need to,' she said. 'Even for you a friend is a friend. You needn't be on the defensive.'

She ran up to the platform. Ceasing to think, he watched the swing of her dark hair against the thin silk of the white blouse, the dark skirt shaping itself to the moving of her limbs. She changed the record. The room filled with a splendid waltz-tune, music with a civilisation behind it, no cheap ragtime, no music-hall. Her body, the white and the black, the pale, serious face softening into laughter, moved with the music. They danced. The white silk was thin under his hand. Her fingers gripped his, her eyes shining. She said breathlessly: 'You haven't for-gotten how.' There was no answer he could make. The music and movement went into his blood. The music, the dance, the dancers melted into unity. Through the window, as they whirled, he saw the river and the long, red bridge. Then the music stopped. The needle grated. He sat down on the steps while she lifted the needle off the record.

'Rita, don't play it again.'

'Why, Peter?'

'I don't want to dance. That's why. I'm tired.'

She came and sat down with him on the steps, a little above him. Eyes fixed on the ground he saw vaguely the dark skirt covering her knees. 'Poor Peter,' she said, 'You work too hard.' Her hand stroked his shoulder. He gripped it, pressed it quietly to his lips, felt her in his arms, as if another man had done a wrong thing and he, Peter Quinn, watched from a prudent, holy distance. She covered her face, leaning against him. He looked down on her dark hair, on the black cloth that covered his own arm encircling the white blouse. His own arm. The thought pressed in on him, filling his mind, crushing him into numbness. Horror at his own weakness sickened him, the yielding to an impulse that brought down in ruin the careful building of four years, discipline, order, resolution, prayer. Was it inherited, in the blood, like Davy's patriotism, in the blood of all men? She raised her head again and he pushed her from him, walking to the window, gripping the painted sill. Over the red bridge the hunt straggled, deserted of foxes, red coats and hungry hounds, riding round fields looking for convenient gates.

'That was terrible,' he said.

She laughed, hiding her fright, shaking her head in a negative that filled him at once with anger and pity, repelling him and attracting him. There was a strange understanding between them, going back to their school-days, to the long sunny afternoons, pigeons fluttering over the old irregular roofs of the town. Wherever they met in time to come they would be allies, in secret alliance, held together by memories of words and actions, by some community of spirit. He hardened himself.

'It was sinful,' he said.

She repeated: 'Sinful.'

'I know it was my fault, Rita. I am what I am. Should have known better. Anything that was between us years ago. All dead now. There's no use in digging up the old skeleton again.'

She stood up, carefully smoothing the dark skirt. 'Why don't you call me names?' she said. 'Say I tempted you. Say I'm the occasion of sin.'

'You didn't.'

Her voice thinned into anger: 'But I did. I wanted you to kiss me. Because I loved you. For years. Even before you went away to be a priest.'

'We were too young.'

'I wasn't. I was old enough to know my mind. I haven't changed. You took yourself away from me.'

'God took me.'

'What had God to do with it? Your own impulse. And deep down in you, you wanted to please your mother, because she was good, a good woman, a good mother.'

'Stop, Rita.'

'You know it's true. I nearly hate you for taking the blame on yourself, for being too deliberately good to see that I led you on.'

'Rita, have sense. You're not that sort.'

'What sort? We're all that sort. But some are afraid and some wouldn't for shame. I'm not afraid. I'm not ashamed. I love you so much I know you better than you know yourself. I know you're out of place where you are. You can't stand back a bit and look at yourself. You're not like the men who make priests, real priests. You're quiet and you read. But that isn't enough. Inside you're different. Maybe it's pride. You're not humble enough to live only with God. You want somebody else to teach you to laugh at yourself. You must find out the poor, laughable way men and women love each other.'

'Stop, Rita.'

'I love you,' she said. 'I love you.'

'You're raving. You don't know what you're saying.'

'Your brother should have been the priest. He's not clever and he's as loud as a saxophone. But there's no pride in him.'

He crossed the room towards the door.

'Are you going, Peter?'

She was sitting weakly on the steps, the anger drained out of her, leaving her frail and crumpled, her white face, white and pitiful, hidden in her hands. At the door he turned and looked at her. He said:

'It's the best thing to do.'

'You won't wait for dinner?'

'I'm not hungry.'

'Daddy will be surprised.'

'Tell him I was in a hurry. I've a lot of calls to make.'

'Will we see you again, Peter?'

'Better not, Rita.'

The tears on her face horrified him. He gripped the door, holding himself where he stood.

'I'm sorry, Peter,' she said. 'I'm sorry.'

'My fault,' he said. He opened the door.

'No,' she said. 'You're proud and silly. But you're not bad. I'm bad. But I'm not as silly as you are.'

There was nothing he could say. He fumbled with the knob of the door, mumbled good-bye.

'Good-bye, Peter. Shall I go to the door?'

'No,' he said. 'I know the way.'

He closed the door behind him, crossed the yard, through the hallway out to the street. The day had darkened. A cold Christmas wind dropped on the pavements the first wet crystals of the coming rain. The red hunters would get wet, forsaken of the foxes, following hares through conveniently opened gates.

Land Without Stars, 1946

THE CHRISTMAS GIFT

Charles Francis Reilly

In the city's dreary back street
Where the glimmering gas lamps glow
Lights the hunger and the squalor
That these gaunt slum dwellers know.

In a dreary, cold, old attic
By the street lamps' misted light,
To a bed that wants surrounding,
A slummer's child repairs to-night.

This the eve of blessed morning,
When the hymn 'Goodwill on Earth',
Ringing o'er the hills all snow clad,
Will recall the Saviour's birth.

Will recall the hillside stable,
Where the ass and oxen's breath,
Saved a Babe – the King of nations –
From the cold wind filled with death.

In the back street of the city,
Where the filths of life abound,
Dreams have filled the infant's sleeping,
Dreams that angels' wreaths surround.

Dreams that waft her from that attic
To a land of magic things,
Where the carol of the angels
O'er each vale in beauty rings.

To a land where want and hunger
Cannot come with heartfelt pangs,
And wherein life's greed and envy
Cannot tear with ugly fangs.

All the beauty seen in dreaming
By a little child asleep,
In a land where guardian angels
Ever o'er her, vigils keep.

Came the dawn upon the mountains
Wrapt in snow on Christmas morn,
All aglitter and agleaming
Are the ices, lakes adorn.

Fell the light upon the city,
Ere from sleep had woke the crowd
Of ill-fated luckless humans,
That the rags of life enshroud.

Crept the ray into the attic
Through the window's dusty pane,
Driving forth the haunting shadows
From the nooks where they remain.

Fell the ray upon the features
Of a little child asleep,
In a land where guardian angels
Ever o'er her, vigils keep.

Features white as snowy marble,
Marble cold when damped by breath;
For the Saviour on His birthday
Had released her soul in death.

Mists of Memory, 1939

CHRISTMAS PREPARATIONS

William Carleton

Christmas Eve, as the day preceding Christmas is called, has been always a day of great preparation and bustle. Indeed, the whole week previous to it is also remarkable, as exhibiting the importance attached by the people to those occasions on which they can give a loose to their love of fun and frolic. The farmhouse undergoes a thorough cleansing. Father and sons are, or rather used to be, all engaged in repairing the out-houses, patching them with thatch where it was wanted, mending mangers, paving stable floors, fixing cow-stakes, making boraghs, removing nuisances, and cleaning streets.

On the other hand, the mothers, daughters, and maids were also engaged in their several departments; the latter scouring the furniture with sand; the mother making culinary preparations, baking bread, killing fowls, or salting meat, whilst the daughters were unusually intent upon the decoration of their own dress, and the making up of the family linen. All, however, was performed with an air of gaiety and pleasure; the ivy and holly were disposed about the dressers and collar beams with great glee; the chimneys were swept amidst songs and laughter; many bad voices, and some good ones, were put in requisition; whilst several, who had never been known to chaunt a stave, alarmed the listeners by the grotesque and incomprehensible nature of their melody. Those who were inclined to devotion – and there is no lack of it in Ireland – took to carols and hymns, which they sang, for want of better airs, to tunes highly comic. We have ourselves often heard the Doxology sung in Irish verse to the facetious air of 'Paudeen O'Rafferty', and other hymns to the tune of 'Peas upon a Trencher', and 'Cruskeen Lawn'. Sometimes, on the contrary, many of them, from the very fulness of jollity, would become pathetic, and indulge in those touching old airs of their country which may be truly called songs of sorrow, from the exquisite and simple pathos with which they abound. This, though it may seem anomalous, is but natural; for there is nothing so apt to recall to the heart those friends, whether absent or dead, with whom it has been connected, as a stated festival. Affection is then awakened, and summons to the hearth where it presides those on whose faces it loves to look. If they be living, it places them in the circle of happiness which surrounds it; and if they be removed for ever from such scenes, their memory, which, amidst the din of ordinary life, has almost passed away, is now restored, and their loss felt as if it had been only just then sustained.

The Midnight Mass, 1833

THE BATTLE OF KINSALE, CHRISTMAS 1601

Rev. E.A. D'Alton

It was at this date that the Spaniards arrived in Ireland. Without guns or ammunition, without means of manufacturing them at home, or ships to replenish their supplies from abroad, the Irish were becoming gradually exhausted, and if left to themselves their resistance should soon necessarily cease. Repeatedly O'Neill and O'Donnell had sought aid from Spain, implored Philip, as the champion of their faith, not to allow a Catholic people to be wiped out. But Philip's movements were slow; and the year 1600 passed by, and the greater part of 1601, and no aid came; nor was it until September of the latter year that the Spaniards set sail. Nor did all who left Spain arrive in Ireland, for a large part under Zubiar got separated from the main body, and only 3,500 arrived at Kinsale. And the choice of Don John Daguilla to command the expedition was unfortunate. He had no sympathy with a revolt; no skill in winning the people to his side; he was impetuous and self-willed, without any skill in forming plans, or any patience in difficulties. He had already commanded in Brittany, but defeats and disasters were all that could be placed to his account, and his incapacity was well established. . .

The intended destination of the Spaniards was Cork; and they first arrived there, borne in forty-five vessels; but the wind suddenly changed, and, unable to land, they put in at Kinsale. The English garrison there evacuated the place on their approach, and when the Spaniards landed they were well received, and were billeted through the town more readily, says Carew, than if they were the Queen's troops. Daguilla published a proclamation that none would be molested, and that whoever wished to leave might do so, taking their goods with them. Carew and Mountjoy were then at Kilkenny. They had been warned from England that the Spaniards were coming, and had gone to Kilkenny to take counsel. Mountjoy proposed returning to Dublin to make his preparations; Carew's advice was that all their forces be at once sent to Munster, his object being to overawe the natives, lest they might join the Spaniards. This advice was taken, and from all quarters the English and their allies flocked to the south. From England 2,000 soldiers came; the Earl of Thomond arrived with 1,000 more; Clanricarde came from Connaught, and Ormond from Kilkenny; the garrisons were withdrawn from Ulster; and by the middle of October, Mountjoy and Carew were in front of Kinsale in command of 12,000 men. . .

The Spaniards in Kinsale grew bold, and night after night sallied from the town; and in these night attacks the English lost many of their men. Their supplies became scarce; they were compelled to keep within their

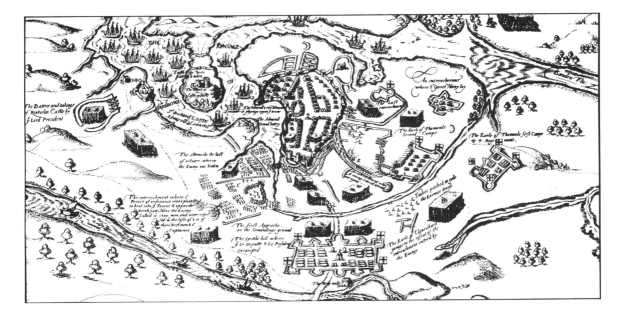

encampments; the winter was severe; the hardships of the campaign told heavily on the troops; the English soldiers especially were sick and weary; dozens died every day; the sentinel was often found dead at his post; desertion became common; the army was rapidly melting away; and by the 20th of December the effective fighting force was reduced to about 6,000 men.

It was at this juncture that O'Neill arrived with 4,000 men and, pitching his camp at Belgooly, besieged the English on the north and east as effectually as O'Donnell had done on the west. All communication with the country round was thus denied the besiegers; the men continued to die from cold and hunger, the horses for want of forage; the numbers who died and were buried within the camp bred sickness among the survivors; only 2,000 English remained; and O'Neill's expectation was that the remainder who were Irish would desert; and his simple, but effective, plan was to continue the siege until the English were exhausted and compelled to surrender. But, unfortunately for himself and for Ireland, his hands were forced. Daguilla had sent urgent letters representing the hardships of his position, and the weakness of the enemy; if the Irish chiefs attacked them from outside he would co-operate from the town, and the result would be certain victory. O'Neill was not convinced, and would still wait, knowing that time was on his side. The Spaniards were in no danger; too much depended on the issue of the contest to run risks; and he foresaw clearly that the defeat of the Irish at Kinsale would be the ruin of their cause. But O'Donnell was for attacking at once. Eight years of victory had given him unbounded self-confidence; he was no longer disposed to adopt the more cautious and wiser advice of O'Neill; and he declared it would be a shame and a disgrace if they did not respond to Daguilla's appeal. At the council of war held there were others as hot-headed as O'Donnell; O'Neill was outvoted, but not convinced, and against his better

59

judgement, preparations were made for attacking the English on the night of the 23rd of December. The Irish troops were good at guerilla warfare, but had no experience in storming entrenchments, and were ill-fitted for such work; and to spoil all their chances, the English were forewarned and, therefore, prepared. For the inevitable Irish traitor who has dogged and ruined every Irish movement was at hand, and a certain Brian MacMahon from Ulster sent the English warning that they were to be attacked. His son, it seems, had been some years before a page to Sir George Carew in England, and for old times' sake he sent a message to Carew for a bottle of whiskey. It was sent, and so grateful was MacMahon that he informed Carew of the meditated attack on the 23rd December. The list of Irish traitors is a long one, but our history records no more infamous transaction than this bartering of faith and country for a bottle of whiskey.

Instead of surprising the enemy, the Irish were themselves surprised. The night was dark and stormy, the guides lost their way; and when they arrived at the English trenches, weary, exhausted, and dispirited, the morning of the 24th had dawned, and they found the English quite ready, horses saddled, men standing to arms. In these circumstances O'Neill's army fell back, intending to defer the attack. They retired in some disorder; the disorder was noted by the enemy; and the Deputy, leaving Carew to watch the Spaniards in the town, took with him 1,200 foot, and 400 horse, and pursued the retreating Irish. The route lay through a boggy glen, cut by a stream at the north-west of the town; and Mountjoy, knowing the capacity both of O'Neill and O'Donnell, was reluctant to pursue them, fearing that they were only enticing him to his ruin. But he was assured that the country beyond was an open and level plain; the Earl of Clanricarde who, with Wingfield, led the cavalry, was especially eager to attack; and when the order was given he fell on the disordered and retreating mass. With some cavalry, O'Donnell drove back the English across the stream, but he was not seconded, and the other Irish chiefs, mounted their horses, and fled like cowards, leaving the infantry to their fate. The rear-guard was driven in upon the main body, and vanguard and rear and main body were soon mixed up together. The Spaniards and Tyrell made a stand, but they were over-whelmed, the larger portion killed, and some, including Ocampo, were taken prisoners. For two miles the pursuit was continued. Clanricarde was especially active, and called out that no Irish were to be spared; the wounded were put to death, and the few prisoners taken were brought into the camp and hanged. The loss on the Irish side is put as high as 2,000 killed and wounded, and as low as 200; but on the English side the loss was small. It was a humiliating day for Ireland, the victory, say the Four Masters, of the few over the many. The defeat is hard to explain. O'Sullivan attributes it to the sins of the Irish, the Four Masters to the anger of God; the mishap of losing their way, and the consequent depression and weariness in the ranks will, only partially account for it; and it is not unlikely that there were other traitors among the chiefs besides MacMahon. Victory would mean their being permanently subject to O'Neill, and like so many other Irish chiefs they perhaps preferred being subject to England. At all events their precipitate and cowardly flight demoralised their followers, and spread a panic through the whole army. Daguilla remained inactive during the battle, and made no sally from the town as he had promised; but, when the battle was over, he sallied to no purpose, and soon after he made terms with the English, and returned to Spain.

History of Ireland from the Earliest Times to the Present Day, 1906

PEACE AND THE GAEL

Padraig H. Pearse

When we are old (those of us who live to be old) we shall tell our grandchildren of the Christmas of 1915 as the second Christmas which saw the nations at war for the freedom of the seas; as the last Christmas, it may be, which saw Ireland, the gate of the seas, in the keeping of the English. For that is the thing for which men are bleeding today in France and Serbia, in Poland and Mesopotamia. The many fight to uphold a tyranny three centuries old, the most arrogant tyranny that there has ever been in the world; and the few fight to break that tyranny. Always it is the many who fight for the evil thing; and always it is the few who win. For God fights with the small battalions. If sometimes it has seemed otherwise, it is because the few who have fought for the good cause have been guilty of some secret faltering, some infidelity to their best selves, some shrinking back in the face of a tremendous duty. . .

War is a terrible thing, but war is not an evil thing. It is the things that make war necessary that are evil. The tyrannies that wars break, the lying formulae that wars overthrow, the hypocrisies that wars strip naked, are evil. Many people in Ireland dread war because they do not know it. Ireland has not known the exhilaration of war for over a hundred years. Yet who will say that she has known the blessings of peace? When war comes to Ireland, she must welcome it as she would welcome the Angel of God. And she will.

It is because peace is so precious a boon that war is so sacred a duty. Ireland will not find Christ's peace until she has taken Christ's sword. What peace she has known in these latter days has been the devil's peace, peace with sin, peace with dishonour. It is a foul thing, dear only to men of foul breeds. Christ's peace is lovely in its coming, beautiful are its feet on the mountains. But it is heralded by terrific messengers; seraphim and cherubim blow trumpets of war before it. We must not flinch when we are passing through that uproar; we must not faint at the sight of blood. Winning through it, we (or those of us who survive) shall come unto great joy. We and our fathers have known the Pax Britannica. To our sons we must bequeath the Peace of the Gael.

Collected Works of Padraig H. Pearse, 1922

A TURN FOR A NEIGHBOUR

Brendan Behan

One Christmas Eve, though not this one nor the one before, there was a man coming in from Cloghran, County Dublin, on a horse and cart to do his Christmas business, selling and buying.

When he got as far as Santry, County Dublin, he remembered that there was an old neighbour dead in a house, so he went in to pay his respects and, after saying that he was sorry for their trouble and all to that effect, he enquired whether he could offer any assistance of a practical nature.

'Well, if it's a thing you wouldn't mind, collecting the coffin; it's ready-measured and made and all; it would be a great help to us.'

'I do not indeed mind carrying the coffin back for you, though I won't be home till a bit late, having to do her shopping. I've a list as long as your arm, of sweets for children, snuff for her old one, rich cake, a jar of malt, two bottles of port wine, snuff for my old one, a collar for the dog, a big red candle to put in the window, a jockey of tobacco for myself, a firkin of porter, two dolls that'll say *Ma-Ma*, one railway train, a jack-in-the-box and a monkey-on-a-stick, two holy pictures, rashers, and black and white pudding and various other combustibles too numerous to mention.

'But I'll stick the coffin up against the rest of them and take the height of good care of it and it'll be me Christmas box and hansel for me poor old neighbour and a good turn for myself because I'll have luck with it.'

So off he went at a jog-trot into the city down from Santry, County Dublin, past Ellenfield and Larkhill, through the big high trees, and the sun just beginning on a feeble attempt to come out, and then having a look at the weather it was in, losing heart, and going back in again, till your man came to Whitehall tram terminus, where they were just getting ready to take the seven o'clock into town.

'Morra, Mick,' shouts a tram fellow, with his mouth full of steam, 'and how's the form?'

'If it was any better,' shouts Mick off the cart, 'I couldn't stick it.'

'More of that to you,' shouts the tram fellow, 'and a happy Christmas, what's more.'

'You, too, and many more along with that,' shouts Mick, and along with him down the Drumcondra Road.

So away he goes into the city, over Binn's Bridge, and into the markets. Before dinner-time he had his selling done and was on to the buying.

He had a good few places to visit, meeting this one and that, but with an

odd adjournment he had everything bought and the coffin collected and on the back of the cart with the rest of the stuff by evening-time. It was dark and cold and the snow starting to come down the back of his neck, but he tightened the collar well round him, and having plenty of the right stuff inside him began a bar of a song for himself, to the tune of 'Haste to the Wedding';

'Twas beyond at Mick Reddin's, at Owen Doyle's weddin',
The lads got the pair of us out for a reel,
Says I, 'Boys, excuse us,' says they, 'don't refuse us,'
'I'll play nice and aisy,' said Larry O'Neill.

Then up we got leppin' it, kickin' and steppin' it,
Herself and myself on the back of the door,
Till Molly, God bless her, fell into the dresser,
And I tumbled over a child on the floor.

Says herself to myself, 'You're as good as the rest,'
Says myself to herself, 'Sure you're better nor gold.'
Says herself to myself, 'We're as good as the best of them,'
'Girl,' says I, 'sure we're time enough old.'

So, with a bit of a song and a mutter of encouragement to the old horse, Mick shortened the way for himself, through snow and dark, till he came to Santry, County Dublin, once again.

There was light and smoke and the sound of glasses and some fellow singing the song of 'The Bould Tenant Farmer' and Mick, being only human, decided to make one last call and pay his respects to the publican.

But getting in was a bit easier than getting out, with drinks coming up from a crowd that was over from the other side of the county, all Doyles, from the hill of Kilmashogue, the Drummer Doyle, the Dandy Doyle, Jowls Doyle, Woodener Doyle, the Dancer Doyle, Elbow Doyle, Altar-

64

boy Doyle, the Hatchet Doyle, Coddle Doyle, the Rebel Doyle, Uncle Doyle, the Shepherd Doyle, Hurrah Doyle and Porternose Doyle.

There was singing and wound opening, and citizens dying for their country on all sides, and who shot the nigger on the Naas Road, and I'm the first man that stuck a monkey in a dustbin and came out without a scratch and there's a man there will prove it, that the lie may choke me, and me country's up and me blood is in me knuckles. 'I don't care a curse now for you, or your queen, but I'll stand by my colour, the harp and the green.'

Till by the time he got on the road again Mick was *maith go leor*, as the man said, but everything went well till he was getting near Cloghran and he had a look round, and there he noticed – the coffin was gone! Gone like Lord Norbury with the divil, as the man said.

Ah, what could he do at all, at all? He sat on the cart for a minute and wondered how he'd face your man if he had to go and tell him that he'd let him down not doing the turn for a family with enough of trouble this Christmas Eve.

Still, looking at it never fattened the pig, so he got off and went back along the road in the direction of the city, and was moseying round in the snow when an RIC man came up from Santry Barracks.

'Come on you, now, and what are you doing walking round this hour of the night?'

'I'm after losing a coffin, Constable,' says Mick.

'They sells desperate bad stuff this time of the year,' sighs the policeman, taking Mick by the arm. 'Come on, my good man, you'll have to come down the road with me now till we instigate investigations into your moves.'

Poor Mick was too disheartened even to resist him, and, sad and sober, he trudged through the snow till they came to the barracks. They went into the dayroom and the constable said to the sergeant, 'I've a fellow here, wandering abroad, and says he's after losing a coffin.'

'He may well have,' says the sergeant, 'because we're after finding one. There it is, standing up behind the door.'

They looked round and Mick's face lit up with joy and relief. 'Praise Him,' said he, running over and throwing his arms round it, 'there it is, me lovely coffin.'

He explained all about it and they let him go off carrying it back to the cart.

'Take better care of it, now,' says the constable and the sergeant from the door.

'I wouldn't have minded,' says Mick, 'only this coffin is not my own. Good night and a happy Christmas to you, and to everyone.'

After the Wake, 1981

11

Here comes I, Oliver Cromwell, as
you may suppose, I conquered many
nations with my copper nose. I made
my foes for to tremble and my enemies

12

for to quake, and beat my opposers till
I made their hearts to ache; and if you
don't believe what I say enter in

Beelzebub, and clear the way. .
Here comes I, Beelzebub, and over
my shoulder I carry my club, and in

THE LAST MUMMER

Seamus Heaney

I

Carries a stone in his pocket,
an ash-plant under his arm.

Moves out of the fog
on the lawn, pads up the terrace,

The luminous screen in the corner
has them charmed in a ring

so he stands a long time behind them.
St. George, Beelzebub and Jack Straw

can't be conjured from mist.
He catches the stick in his fist

and, shrouded, starts beating
the bars of the gate.

His boots crack the road. The stone
clatters down off the slates.

II

He came trammelled
in the taboos of the country

picking a nice way through
the long toils of blood

and feuding.
His tongue went whoring

among the civil tongues,
he had an eye for weather-eyes

at cross-roads and lane-ends
and could don manners

at a flutter of curtains.
His straw mask and hunch were fabulous

disappearing beyond the lamplit
slabs of a yard.

III

You dream a cricket in the hearth
and cockroach on the floor,

a line of mummers
marching out the door

as the lamp flares in the draught.
Melted snow off their feet

leaves you in peace.
Again an old year dies

on your hearthstone, for good luck.
The moon's host elevated

in a monstrance of holly trees,
he makes dark tracks, who had

untousled a first dewy path
into the summer grazing.

Wintering Out, 1972

CHRISTMAS IN LECALE, 1602

Josias Bodley

Captain Josias Bodley, brother of the founder of the Bodleian Library at Oxford, was an officer in the army sent by Queen Elizabeth to punish Hugh O'Neill, Earl of Tyrone, for revolting from his allegiance in 1595. The redoubtable captain had four rather rough years campaigning in Ireland before he received an invitation to spend the Christmas of 1602 with Sir Richard Morrison at Downpatrick, in the barony of Lecale, County Down. A MSS account of his visit is preserved in the great library at Oxford and provides one of the most complete pictures of the social life of the period. The extract below gives an account of the Christmas week's festivities enjoyed by the captain and his friends, one of whom (Captain Toby Caulfield) was the founder of the house of Charlemont.

Good God! What have I taken on me to do? Truly I am an ass, otherwise I would never have undertaken so heavy a burden; but no matter, I shall do what I can. . .

I have taken in hand to recount what happened in a journey which Captain Caulfield, Captain Jephson and I, made to Lecale, to visit our friend Sir Richard Morrison, and divert ourselves there. And I shall narrate everything in due order. . .

The aforesaid Master Morrison sent very kind letters to us, inviting us to keep the Nativity, (which the English call 'Christmas') with him. We set out for the town commonly called Newry, which was one day's journey. There, to speak the truth, we were not very well entertained, nor according to our qualities; for that town produces nothing but lean beef, and very rarely mutton; the very worst wine; nor was there any bread, except biscuits, even in the Governor's house. However, we did our best to be merry and jocund with the bad wine, putting sugar in it, (as the senior lawyers are used to do, with Canary wine) – with toasted bread, which in English is called 'a lawyer's nightcap'. There we found Captain Adderton, an honest fellow and a friend of ours who having nothing to do was easily persuaded to accompany us to Lecale.

So the next morning we four take horse and set out. We had no guide except Captain Caulfield, who promised he would lead us very well. But before we had ridden three miles we lost our way and were compelled to go on foot, leading our horses through bogs and marshes, which was very troublesome; and some of us were not wanting who swore silently between our teeth, and wished our guide at a thousand devils. At length we came to some village of obscure name, where, for two brass shillings, we brought with us a countryman who might lead us to the Island of Magennis, ten miles distant from the town of Newry: for Master Morrison had promised he would meet us there.

The weather was very cold, and it began to roar dreadfully with a strong wind in our faces, when we were on the mountains, where there was neither tree nor house; but there was no remedy save patience. Captain Bodley alone had a long cloak, with a hood, into which he prudently thrust his head, and laughed somewhat into himself to see the others so badly armed against the storm.

We now came to the island of Magennis, where, alighting from our horses, we met Master Morrison and Captain Constable; with many others, whom, for the sake of brevity, I pass by. They had tarried there at least three hours. expecting our arrival; and in the mean time, drank ale and usquebaugh. . .

It was ten or twelve miles from that island to Downpatrick, where Master Morrison dwelt; and the way seemed much longer on account of our wish to be there. At length, as all things have an end, and a black pudding two (as the proverb hath it) we came by little and little to the said house. And now began that more than Lucullan entertainment. . .

When we had approached within a stone's throw of the house, – or rather palace – of the said Master Morrison – behold! forthwith innumerable servants! some light us with pinewood lights and torches because it is dark; others, as soon as we alight, take our horses, and lead them into a handsome and spacious stable, where neither hay nor oats are wanting. Master Morrison himself leads us by wide stairs into a large hall where a fire is burning the height of our chins, as the saying is; and afterwards into a bed-chamber, prepared in the Irish fashion. . .

In an hour we heard some one down in the kitchen calling with a loud voice 'To the Dresser'. Forthwith we see a long row of servants, decently dressed, each with dishes of the most select meats, which they place on the table in the very best style. One presents to us a silver basin with the most limpid water; another hands us a very white towel; others arrange chairs and seats in their proper places. – 'What need of words, let us be seen in action,' – (as Ajax says in Ovid). Grace having been said we begin to fix our eyes intently on the dishes, whilst handling our knives: and here you might have plainly seen those Belgian feasts, where, at the beginning is silence, in the middle the cranching of teeth, and at the end the chattering of the people. For at first we sat as if rapt and astounded by the variety of meats and dainties.

But after a short time we fall to roundly on every dish, calling now and then for wine, now and then for attendance, everyone according to his whim. In the midst of supper Master Morrison ordered be given to him a glass goblet full of claret, which measured (as I conjecture) ten or eleven inches roundabout, and drank to the health of all, and to our happy arrival. We freely received it from him, thanking him and drinking, one after the other, as much as he drank before us. He then gave four or five healths of the chief men, and of our absent friends. . . And it is a very praiseworthy thing, and has perhaps more in it than any one would believe; and there was not one among us who did pledge him and each other without any scruple or gainsay, which I was very glad to see; for it was a proof of unanimity and assured friendship. . .

The supper, (which, as I have said, was most elegant) being ended, we again enter our bed-room, in which was a large fire, (for at the time it was exceedingly cold out of doors) and benches for sitting on; and plenty of tobacco, with nice pipes, was set before us. The wine also had begun to operate a little on us. . . I need not tell how soundly we slept till morning, for that is easily understood, all things considered; at least if the old syllogism be true: 'He who drinks well sleeps well.' When the sun had already made almost the fourth part of his daily journey above our horizon, and the domestics knowing that it was time for us to rise, came in to light the fire, we all suddenly awoke, and saluted each other. . . Before we get out of bed they bring to us a certain aromatic of strong ale, compounded with sugar and eggs, to comfort and strengthen the stomach; they also bring beer, (if any prefer it) with toasted bread and nutmeg to allay thirst, steady the head, and cool the liver; they also bring pipes of the best tobacco to drive away rheums and catarrhs.

We now all jump quickly out of bed, put on our clothes, approach the fire, and when all are ready, walk abroad together to take the air, which, in that region, is most salubrious and delightful, so that if I wished to enumerate all the advantages of the place, not only powers (of description) but time itself be wanting. I shall therefore omit that, as being already known, and revert to ourselves, who, having now had a sufficient walk, returned to our lodging as dinner-time was at hand.

But how can we now tell about the sumptuous preparation of everything? How about the dinners? How about the suppers? How about the dainties? For we seemed as if present, (as you would suppose) at the nuptial banquet to which some Cleopatra had invited her Antony; so many varieties of meats were there, so many kinds of condiments; about every one of which I would willingly say something, only that I fear being tedious. I shall therefore demonstrate, from a single dinner, what may be imagined of the rest. There was a large and beautiful collar of brawn, with its accompaniments, to wit, mustard and Muscadel wine; there were well-stuffed geese, (such as the Lord Bishop is wont to eat at Ardbraccan) the legs of which Captain Caulfield always laid hold of for himself; there were pies of venison and of various kinds of game; pasties also, some of marrow, with innumerable plums; others of it with coagulated milk, – such as the Lord Mayor and Aldermen of London almost always have at their feasts; others, which they call Tarts, of divers shapes, materials and colours, made of beef, mutton and veal. I do not mention, because they are reckoned vulgar, other kinds of dishes, wherein France much abounds, and which they designate 'Quelq'choses'. Neither do I relate anything of the delicacies which accompanied the cheese, because they would exceed all belief. I may say in one word, that all things were there supplied us most luxuriously and most copiously.

And lest any one might think that God had sent us the meat, but the Devil the cook (as the proverb says) there was a cook there so expert in his art that his equal could scarce be found; and I shall now say one *big* word, – I believe that Master Robert, the cook who presides over the kitchen of the Lord Deputy, (with pardon be it spoken) is not a much better cook, or more skilled in his art, than he – and his name is Philip. And truly this may suffice as to the dishes and dainties – for a word is enough to the wise.

Ulster Journal of Archaeology, 1854

A FOURTEENTH-CENTURY CAROL

Alfred Perceval Graves

When God came down on Earth to dwell,
Great cold befell:
Yet Mary on the road hath seen
A fig-tree green.
Said Joseph: 'O Mary, let the fruit hang;
For thirty good mile we have still to gang,
Lest we be late!'

When Mary unto a village door
At last did win,
She thus bespake the cottager:
'Sir, take us in!
Since for this young Child's tender sake
A pitying heart must surely ache,
The night's so cold.'

'You're welcome all to my ox-stall!'
The good man cried.
But in the middle of the night
He rose and sighed:
'Where are ye now, poor hapless ones?
That ye're not frozen to the bones,
I marvel much.'

Then back into his house he runs
From forth the byre –
'Rouse up, rouse up, my dearest wife,
And light a fire,
As fine as ever sent up smoke,
Whereat these poor and perishing folk
May comfort them.'

Mary with joy into the house
The Babe has brought,
Joseph her just and faithful spouse,
His wallet sought.
Therefrom he took a kettle small;
Some snow the Child therein let fall,
An lo 'tis flour!

Thereto the Babe has added ice;
'Tis sugar straight!
Now water drops, and, in a trice,
'Tis milk most sweet!
The kettle, fast as you could look,
They hung upon the kitchen hook
A meal to cook.

The godly Joseph carved a spoon
From out a brand;
To ivory it changed full soon
And adamant.
When Mary gave the Babe the food,
He became Jesus, Son of God.
Before their eyes.

A Celtic Psaltery, 1917

from THE DEAD

James Joyce

It was always a great affair, the Misses Morkan's annual dance. Everybody who knew them came to it, members of the family, old friends of the family, the members of Julia's choir, any of Kate's pupils that were grown up enough, and even some of Mary Jane's pupils too. Never once had it fallen flat. For years and years it had gone off in splendid style, as long as anyone could remember: ever since Kate and Julia, after the death of their brother Pat, had left the house in Stoney Batter and taken Mary Jane, their only niece, to live with them in the dark, gaunt house on Usher's Island, the upper part of which they had rented from Mr Fulham, the corn-factor on the ground floor. That was a good thirty years ago if it was a day. Mary Jane, who was then a little girl in short clothes, was now the main prop of the household, for she had the organ in Haddington Road. She had been through the Academy and gave a pupils' concert every year in the upper room of the Antient Concert Rooms. Many of her pupils belonged to the better-class families on the Kingstown and Dalkey line. Old as they were, her aunts also did their share. Julia, though she was quite grey, was still the leading soprano in Adam and Eve's, and Kate, being too feeble to go about much, gave music lessons to beginners on the old square piano in the back room. Lily, the caretaker's daughter, did housemaid's work for them. Though their life was modest, they believed in eating well; the best of everything: diamond-bone sirloins, three-shilling tea and the best bottled stout. But Lily seldom made a mistake in the orders, so that she got on well with her three mistresses. They were fussy, that was all. But the only thing they would not stand was back answers.

Of course, they had good reason to be fussy on such a night. And then it was long after ten o'clock and yet there was no sign of Gabriel and his wife. Besides they were dreadfully afraid that Freddy Malins might turn up screwed. They would not wish for worlds that any of Mary Jane's pupils should see him under the influence; and when he was like that it was sometimes very hard to manage him. Freddy Malins always came late, but they wondered what could be keeping Gabriel: and that was what brought them every two minutes to the banisters to ask Lily had Gabriel or Freddy come.

'O, Mr Conroy,' said Lily to Gabriel when she opened the door for him, 'Miss Kate and Miss Julia thought you were never coming. Good night, Mrs Conroy.'

'I'll engage they did,' said Gabriel, 'but they forget that my wife here takes three mortal hours to dress herself.'

He stood on the mat, scraping the snow from his goloshes, while Lily led his wife to the foot of the stairs and called out:

'Miss Kate, here's Mrs Conroy.'

Kate and Julia came toddling down the dark stairs at once. Both of them kissed Gabriel's wife, said she must be perished alive, and asked was Gabriel with her.

'Here I am as right as the mail, Aunt Kate! Go on up. I'll follow,' called out Gabriel from the dark.

He continued scraping his feet vigorously while the three women went upstairs, laughing, to the ladies' dressing-room. A light fringe of snow lay like a cape on the shoulders of his overcoat and like toecaps on the toes of his goloshes; and, as the buttons of his overcoat slipped with a squeaking noise through the snow-stiffened frieze, a cold, fragrant air from out-of-doors escaped from crevices and folds.

'Is it snowing again, Mr Conroy?' asked Lily.

She had preceded him into the pantry to help him off with his overcoat. Gabriel smiled at the three syllables she had given his surname and glanced at her. She was a slim, growing girl, pale in complexion and with hay-coloured hair. The gas in the pantry made her look still paler. Gabriel had known her when she was a child and used to sit on the lowest step nursing a rag doll.

'Yes, Lily,' he answered, 'and I think we're in for a night of it.'

He looked up at the pantry ceiling, which was shaking with the stamping and shuffling of feet on the floor above, listened for a moment to the piano and then glanced at the girl, who was folding his overcoat carefully at the end of a shelf.

'Tell me, Lily,' he said in a friendly tone, 'do you still go to school?'

'O no, sir,' she answered. 'I'm done schooling this year and more.'

'O, then,' said Gabriel gaily, 'I suppose we'll be going to your wedding one of these fine days with your young man, eh?'

The girl glanced back at him over her shoulder and said with great bitterness:

'The men that is now is only all palaver and what they can get out of you.'

Gabriel coloured, as if he felt he had made a mistake and, without looking at her, kicked off his goloshes and flicked actively with his muffler at his patent-leather shoes.

He was a stout, tallish young man. The high colour of his cheeks pushed upwards even to his forehead, where it scattered itself in a few formless patches of pale red; and on his hairless face there scintillated restlessly the polished lenses and the bright gilt rims of the glasses which screened his delicate and restless eyes. His glossy black hair was parted in the middle and brushed in a long curve behind his ears where it curled slightly beneath the groove left by his hat.

When he had flicked lustre into his shoes he stood up and pulled his waistcoat down more tightly on his plump body. Then he took a coin rapidly from his pocket.

'O Lily,' he said, thrusting it into her hands, 'it's Christmas-time, isn't it? Just. . . here's a little. . .'

He walked rapidly towards the door.

'O no, sir!' cried the girl, following him. 'Really, sir, I wouldn't take it.'

'Christmas-time! Christmas-time!' said Gabriel, almost trotting to the stairs and waving his hand to her in deprecation.

The girl, seeing that he had gained the stairs, called out after him: 'Well, thank you, sir.'

He waited outside the drawing-room door until the waltz should finish, listening to the skirts that swept against it and to the shuffling of feet. He was still discomposed by the girl's bitter and sudden retort. It had cast a gloom over him which he tried to dispel by arranging his cuffs and the bows of his tie. He then took from his waistcoat pocket a little paper and glanced at the headings he had made for his speech. He was undecided about the lines from Robert Browning, for he feared they would be above the heads of his hearers. Some quotation that they would recognize from Shakespeare or from the Melodies would be better. The indelicate clacking of the men's heels and the shuffling of their soles reminded him that their grade of culture differed from his. He would only make himself ridiculous by quoting poetry to them which they could not understand. They would think that he was airing his superior education. He would fail with them just as he had failed with the girl in the pantry. He had taken up a wrong tone. His whole speech was a mistake from first to last, an utter failure. . .

Dubliners, 1914

THE MUMMER SPEAKS

John Montague

'God save our shadowed lands
Stalked by this night beast of the dead
– Turnip roundness of the skull,
Sockets smouldering in the head –
Will no St George or Patrick come,
Restore to us our once blessed
And blossoming, now barren home?'

He paused on the threshold,
Clashed his sword of wood,
His swinging lantern on the snow
Three blood-red circles where he stood;
Herded listeners gaped
Like goslings, as if they understood.

Bold as brass, a battering knight
Came roaring through the door,
Bussed the ladies on his right,
Smashed the devil to the floor.
Justice triumphs on the spot,
With straw, like guts, strewn everywhere;
False Satan struts no more.

Seen in womblike darkness,
Two wearing decades ago;
From which I still recall
Their faces like listening animals,
A stormlamp swinging to and fro,
And from those creaking country rhymes,
That purging láment of bad times.

Poisoned Lands, 1961

CHRISTMAS MORNING

Frank O'Connor

Coming on to dawn, I woke with the feeling that something dreadful had happened. The whole house was quiet, and the little bedroom that looked out on the foot and a half of back yard was pitch-dark. It was only when I glanced at the window that I saw how all the silver had drained out of the sky. I jumped out of bed to feel my stocking, well knowing that the worst had happened. Santa had come while I was asleep, had gone away with an entirely false impression of me, because all he had left me was some sort of book, folded up, a pen and pencil, and a tuppenny bag of sweets. Not even Snakes-and-Ladders! For a while I was too stunned even to think. A fellow who was able to drive over rooftops and climb down chimneys without getting stuck – God, wouldn't you think he'd know better?

Then I began to wonder what that foxy boy, Sonny, had. I went to his side of the bed and felt his stocking. For all his spelling and sucking-up he hadn't done so much better, because, apart from a bag of sweets like mine, all Santa had left him was a pop-gun, one that fired a cork on a piece of string and which you could get in any huxter's shop for six-pence.

All the same, the fact remained that it was a gun, and a gun was better than a book any day of the week. The Dohertys had a gang, and the gang fought the Strawberry Lane kids who tried to play football on our road. That gun would be very useful to me in many ways, while it would be lost on Sonny who wouldn't be let play with the gang, even if he wanted to.

Then I got the inspiration, as it seemed to me, direct from heaven. Suppose I took the gun and gave Sonny the book! Sonny would never be any good in the gang: he was fond of spelling, and a studious child like him could learn a lot of spellings from a book like mine. As he hadn't seen Santa any more than I had, what he hadn't seen wouldn't grieve him. I was doing no harm to anyone; in fact, if Sonny only knew, I was doing him a good turn which he might have cause to thank me for later. That was one thing I was always keen on; doing good turns. Perhaps this was Santa's intention the whole time and he had merely become confused between us. It was a mistake that might happen to anyone. So I put the book, the pencil, and the pen into Sonny's stocking and the popgun into my own, and returned to bed and slept again. As I say, in those days I had plenty of initiative.

It was Sonny who woke me, shaking me to tell me that Santa had come and left me a gun. I let on to be surprised and rather disappointed in the gun, and to divert his mind from it made him show me his picture book, and cracked it up to the skies.

As I knew, that kid was prepared to believe anything, and nothing would do him then but to take the presents in to show Father and Mother. This was a bad moment for me. After the way she had behaved about the langing [playing truant], I distrusted Mother, though I had the consolation of believing that the only person who could contradict me was now somewhere up by the North Pole. That gave me a certain confidence, so Sonny and I burst in with our presents, shouting: 'Look what Santa Claus brought!'

Father and Mother woke, and Mother smiled, but only for an instant. As she looked at me her face changed. I knew that look; I knew it only too well. It was the same she had worn the day I came home from langing, when she said I had no word.

'Larry,' she said in a low voice, 'where did you get that gun?'

'Santa left it in my stocking, Mummy,' I said, trying to put on an injured air, though it baffled me how she guessed that he hadn't. 'He did, honest.'

'You stole it from that poor child's stocking while he was asleep,' she said, her voice quivering with indignation. 'Larry, Larry, how could you be so mean?'

'Now, now, now,' Father said deprecatingly, ''tis Christmas morning.'

'Ah,' she said with real passion, 'it's easy it comes to you. Do you think I want my son to grow up a liar and a thief?'

'Ah, what thief, woman?' he said testily. 'Have sense, can't you?' He was as cross if you interrupted him in his benevolent moods as if they were of the other sort, and this one was probably exacerbated by a feeling of guilt for his behaviour of the night before. 'Here, Larry,' he said, reaching out for the money on the bedside table, 'here's sixpence for you and one for Sonny. Mind you don't lose it now!'

But I looked at Mother and saw what was in her eyes. I burst out crying, threw the popgun on the floor, and ran bawling out of the house before anyone on the road was awake. I rushed up the lane behind the house and threw myself on the wet grass.

I understood it all, and it was almost more than I could bear; that there was no Santa Claus, as the Dohertys said, only Mother trying to scrape together a few coppers from the housekeeping; that Father was mean and common and a drunkard, and that she had been relying on me to raise her out of the misery of the life she was leading. And I knew that the look in her eyes was the fear that, like my father, I should turn out to be mean and common and a drunkard.

The Stories of Frank O'Connor, 1953

CLEW BAY.

CHRISTMAS IN THE WEST OF IRELAND

Sophie O'Brien

Our first Christmas in Westport has remained clear in my memory after forty years. I still feel the delightful bracing air on my face, with the vivifying breath of the mountain and of the sea.

We lived two miles out of Westport, by the seashore – not an open sea, but a dear little bay, where the tide came in joyously, and yet we were sheltered from the fierce breeze and storms of Old Head, by a belt of mountains that stretched on both sides of the bay and spread their protecting arms around Mallow Cottage.

On Christmas Eve we went to town, and dear Father McDermot heard our Confession. First Mass was at seven. In my ignorance I ordered the outside car that was to bring us to Mass at half-past six. It was a clear frosty morning. There was a glow of mysterious light, the morning star was shining in the East and giving out *cette obscure clarté qui tombe des étoiles.* We went up the quay road. The domain must have been closed, whether it was too early, or whatever the reason must have been. The way through the domain – as Lord Sligo's park was called – was beautifully wooded. It was much quicker, being level, while the quay road was rough and went up and down, in a way that was hard on horse or man. Of course, when one returned from Westport, along the quay road, one came to a spot from which one's eyes soared over a lovely panorama of mountain and sea and islands. Thackeray, in his Irish sketch-book, described the scene with marvellous accuracy. Any one taking up the volume and reading the description will feel a glow of enthusiasm only to be equalled or increased by witnessing the scene.

But when one went towards Westport by the quay road it was

another story. It was a dull drive and a slow one. On that Christmas morning we had not realised how very early we ought to have been at the Church door to get a chance of coming in.

When we arrived a couple of minutes before Mass began, the very doors were thronged with worshippers, and there was not a place for a pin's head in all the Church. We were looking disconsolately around, when one of the priests came along and saw our sad plight. He beckoned us to follow him to a side door, and brought us to a quiet spot where we knelt, with other lucky ones, who had been rescued from despair by the same kind priest.

It was the first time I witnessed a scene of such devout recollection and religious enthusiasm as was enacted on that winter morning by the western worshippers, and my heart joined in the joyous celebration with a gratitude that years and distance have not diminished.

Somehow it seemed that never before had I come so near the Divine Babe and His Holy Mother as in this poor Mayo Church, amidst the very poor people all around – poor in this world's wealth, but rich in hope and faith and charity.

The West of Ireland in those days – forty years ago – was a very poor place indeed. As we lived in Mallow Cottage we came to know intimately the lives of our neighbours in city and country, and the amount of misery borne with courage and resignation that I came to know, filled me with awed admiration.

On that Christmas morning, I little knew how far some of the worshippers had to walk to be in time for Mass. I had been proud of ourselves for being ready at half-past six. I realised when too late that we ought to have left the house at six to be in time, and even then that would have meant little hardship, when we could drive, compared to what others had to go through. Many of those who filled the body of the church had walked long distances in the dark, fasting, and thought nothing of it.

In those days, in the Westport Church, there were only a few benches near the confessionals, and in the body of the church the congregation knelt on the flags or stood. There were no seats. How well one prayed under those conditions! Is it an old woman's imagination – apt to gild the past with the glamour of her youthful dreams – that the more uncomfortable the body was, the more absorbed in prayer grew the spirit? One felt somewhat stiff and sore, when one stood up, it is true, but there was a joyous feeling of having been near the Holy of Holies for a short spell. One seemed to bring away from that Christmas Mass a feeling of joy that made the whole day a very happy one, in our ltitle Mayo cottage where so many of our friends thought we would feel out of the world.

The Irish Monthly, 1931

A CHISELLER'S CHRISTMAS

Eamon Mac Thomais

We may not have been able to count the weeks or months to Easter or Whit, or even to St Patrick's Day, but we always knew when it was only twelve weeks to Christmas. Clarke's sweet and toy shop at the top of Bulfin Road had both windows full of a vast selection of toys. Each item had its own label, telling its own story.

A red fire engine with a yellow ladder: three shillings (or twelve weeks at threepence per week and it's yours on Christmas Eve). A swarm of children, with our noses stuck to the glass window and our warm breaths in the cold October air fogging up the window panes. Then polishing the window with the sleeves of our coats and listening to the chorus of voices all shouting –

'I'm getting that, and that, and maybe I'll get that, but I'm defney getting that.'

Only for Clarke's twelve-weeks-to-Christmas plan many's a child in Inchicore and Kilmainham would never have seen a toy on Christmas morning. We seldom missed a Sunday's visit as the shop was only a few paces from St Michael's Church, and even on a weekday a special visit would be made just to see again the toys we dreamed would be in our stockings at the foot of the bed on Christmas morning.

On Christmas Eve, the girl next door would come in to help me write my letter to Santa Claus. She would dictate the letter and address the envelope, but when she insisted that I put down a blue sports racing car with the number of my hall door (30) on it, I threw down the pencil.

'I want a red fire engine with a yellow ladder,' I said. 'I don't want a blue racing car, even if it has our hall door number on it.'

God bless Bernie, she's a Poor Clare nun today in Belfast, but she had great patience in those days. The battle between the blue racing car and the red fire engine was not won that Christmas Eve as I ran upstairs saying I was going to wait up all night and if Mister Santa Claus tried to off-load his old blue racing car into my stocking I'd give him a good kick.

I remember fighting the sandman that night. The sandman was the man (invisible) who went around at night time throwing sand into your eyes to make you sleep or blind you. But the sandman had won the battle and when I awoke the next morning there was the bloody blue racing car sticking out of my stocking at the end of the bed. I cursed Santa a few times and then noticed the little mouth organ and the sweets in the other stocking. I was told later that this was Santa's way of saying 'sorry', that he must have had only one red fire engine and that he had given it to a poor little boy with no mammy or daddy.

'After all, you have a mammy, even if you have no daddy.'

'That's true,' I said and began to think of what my pal had said to me a few days before Christmas: 'You're lucky. You may have no daddy but you have three mammies.' He was referring to my Ma and her two sisters, my aunts who lived with us.

'And besides,' he added, 'mammies are always better than daddies. Sure I never see mine only when he comes home drunk and tries to beat us all up.'

'The Ma and the aunts never get drunk,' I said, 'But I still get bet up, now and again, when I'm bold.'

After Mass that Christmas morning I rushed over to Clarke's toy shop. Both windows were empty. The red fire engine with the yellow ladder was gone. Old Mrs. Clarke, Lord rest her, told me that Santa had collected all the toys last night and she didn't know where the poor little boy lived who had got the fire engine.

I think that was the only Christmas that I was disappointed. The following year I got the red fire engine with the yellow ladder and I wondered if the poor little boy got the blue racing car.

Gur Cake and Coal Blocks, 1976

CHRISTMAS IN 'THE BIG HOUSE'

Elizabeth Hamilton

Christmas Day between tea and bedtime. The light from a standard lamp makes a soft amber glow, while on the mantelshelf candles in silver candlesticks pick out the holly berries among their shining leaves. My father bends over me. He is wearing a dark suit and the high white collar. 'Surely you wouldn't hide anything from me?' he says as I try ineffectually to conceal with my hands the broken rein belonging to the toy horse, almost as tall as myself, which was my parents' present to me. The words were spoken not in reproach but surprise; friend speaking to friend. I had no cause to fear my father – I do not suppose anyone has been blessed with a more gentle father. I was trying to hide the rein (it had snapped a moment before) not because I was afraid, but because I was overawed by the solemnity of the day. Christmas Day was one of those times when it was required that everything be perfect: one felt instinctively that gifts must be flawless, if only that the donor be well pleased. This imposed upon the day, wonderful though it was, a certain constraint. It was much the same on birthdays – and to a lesser degree Sundays, anniversaries and indeed any day that might be regarded as being in the nature of a 'special occasion'. To be naughty at such a time was to cloud the day for everyone. I remember my fifth birthday – the storm that broke after lunch. All because I wanted, there and then, to give to Mrs Connolly – who came to help in the kitchen and was leaving to go home – a slice of the iced birthday cake my mother had made me. I must not, I was told; it would spoil the appearance of the cake for the afternoon when visitors were coming to tea. Bewildered by the illogicality of the adult world – at one moment I was told to give away my possessions, at the next forbidden to do so – I flew into a paroxysm of rage.

Apart from the broken rein I remember the present of the toy horse for another reason. It is a memory of disillusionment; reality falling short of fantasy. And with this a sense of isolation – for the delicacy of the occasion forbade me to speak of my disappointment. The horse I had pictured during the weeks of waiting that preceded Christmas had a sleek coat of real skin – like the coat of Lady, the chestnut mare. The horse that confronted me when I tore off the wrapping on Christmas morning was covered not with skin but chocolate-brown felt. It had no sheen, no life.

If the expected can prove sometimes to be a disappointment, equally there are occasions when the unexpected provides pleasure to a degree that may seem out of all proportion to the source. The toy cow (it was not more than a couple of inches high) that my aunt Grace gave me another Christmas filled me with a delight that knew no bounds. I could not have enough of stroking the silky coat, feeling with my fingers the curves and angles of the body, the neat hooves, the tasselled bootlace tail. It was as near as could be in miniature to the one Jersey cow that grazed on the lawn along with the black-and-white Friesians, the blue-black Kerries, the white-masked Herefords and the strawberry roans.

Another Christmas I was given a musical box made of silvery metal striped with blue and crimson and emerald. When I wound it to the full, the handle used to give a jerk – a backward leap, as if to show there was a limit to what might be asked of it. It played a repertoire of little thin tinkling tunes that one after another came to a sudden stop, leaving the listener as it were suspended. All the gaiety and all the sadness of the world were contained in those tinkling tunes.

Another year a Christmas party was given by our neighbour Mrs Tottenham. It was at her, when she came to tea one day, that I flung the knife across the table, not because I disliked her (she was friendly, kindly, gay, always laughing) but because I was enraged by the ostrich plumes nodding on her hat – still more by the fact that she was absorbing my mother's attention.

At the party there were children who rarely, if ever, saw one another from one year's end to the next. They had come great distances in pony-traps and dog-carts, broughams and landaus, cabs and side-cars. On the gravel outside Woodstock wheels scrunched, horses stamped and snorted. The Palladian frontage of the house stood up out of the dusk. A liveried footman was on the steps. In the hall a blaze of lights picked out the stuccoed Adam ceiling, Ionic pilasters, the sweep of the staircase, the full-length portrait of 'Tottenham in his Boots' – Charles Tottenham who in the year 1731, when a bill was to be debated in Dublin to make over a surplus £60,000 to the British Government, took horse and riding through the night presented himself in Parliament House, despite the protests of the serjeant-at-arms, without waiting to change out of his mud-spattered riding kit.

The huge drawing-room, resplendent with gilded furnishings, crimson hangings and Empire figures supporting torches, rang with the voices and laughter of children. There were little boys in velvet suits with silver buttons, older boys in Eton jackets. Some of the girls wore velvet dresses, others muslin, with a sash tied into a stiff bow. They eyed one another (or so it seemed to me) suspiciously, like cats meeting for the first time. We played Postman's Knock and Musical Chairs, Blind Man's Buff and Hunt the Slipper. We pulled crackers made of crinkled scarlet paper laced with silver, containing caps and trinkets and charms. As the name of each one of us was called we were presented with a gift from a Christmas tree so tall that its top was lost among a glitter of chandeliers.

An Irish Childhood, 1963

CHRISTMAS IN OLD DUBLIN 2

Annie M.P. Smithson

In 1689, we again see Dublin Castle at Christmastide. But now the scene is very different. The great State apartments are blazing with light, hundreds of candles shedding their illumination around, while everywhere is heard the sound of music and dancing. James II – weakest of all the Stuart Kings – is keeping Christmas here. We can believe the splendour of those Christmas festivities. James, poor-spirited and vacillating as he proved himself to be, must still have possessed his share of the well-known Stuart charm, and we may be sure that the Irish Jacobites flocked to do homage at his Court during those days of gaiety, when he little knew what Fate held in store for him, when he would go forth to meet the Dutchman at the Boyne.

And now we see Ireland entering upon the long night of the Penal days, and we may imagine that the greeting, 'A Merry Christmas!' would then be seldom heard from the lips of the persecuted people.

Dublin has often been in the grip of great frosts at Christmastime. In the year 1739, in the month of December, a severe frost set in which lasted until the following February. It was so severe that it caused the potatoes and other vegetables to be unfit for food, and also destroyed trees and plants. It was said to have frozen the earth to the depth of nine inches. The Liffey was frozen over and the citizens amused themselves on the ice. The sheep and birds died in thousands, and the sufferings of the poor – whose staple diet then and much later was the potato – must have been intense. Dublin, however, has always found citizens in plenty to show a practical sympathy with the unfortunate, and in *Faulkner's Journal*, in Jan., 1740, we catch a glimpse of the kindness of a Dublin clergyman, a close friend of Dean Swift, as follows: 'The Revd. Dr. Delany, who hath long been accustomed to divide two Beeves, with several Loaves of Bread every Christmas, amongst the neighbouring Poor about Glasnevin, hath this Year given three, and resolves to have one killed every Week for that Purpose, while the hard Weather continues.'

Another severe frost commenced on Christmas Day of the year 1783, and it lasted, without any sign of a thaw, until Feb. 21st, 1784.

The Dublin Christmas which will be remembered as the time of the greatest musical event in our city's history is that of 1741. Handel was visiting Dublin, and gave a series of concerts. Here is the reference in *Faulkner's Journal* to his first concert:-

Last Wednesday, [23rd December] Mr. Handel had his first Oratorio at Mr. Neal's Musick Hall in Fishamble Street, which was crowded with a more numerous and polite Audience than was ever seen upon the like Occasion. The Performance was superior to anything of the kind in the Kingdom before; and our Nobility and Gentry, to shew their taste for all kinds of Genius, expressed their great satisfaction, and have already given all imaginable Encouragement to this grand Musick.

In the following January, Handel gave his great concert in aid of Mercer's Hospital, and soon after, in April, produced the *Messiah*. His masterpiece is now a part of our Christmas celebrations, for at that season it is sung in our churches and at concerts not only in Dublin but all over the Christian world.

What was a Dublin Christmas like about a century ago? No doubt the shops made as great a display as possible with all the brightness their proprietors could command.

The lighting of the city was by gas; this had been first done in 1825, but there were as yet no gas mantles and the illuminations could not have been very good. In private houses the lighting was still by lamps and candles. Ladies wore little bonnets and muffs and had tight waists. They stayed at home in the evenings, knitting and sewing, and listening while their lords and masters stood on the hearthrug laying down the law about everything, the wives just replying, 'Yes, dear!' and 'No, dear!' and 'Of course *you* know best, my love!' – all the time probably knowing that the dear man was talking very foolishly.

Christmas was kept quietly in some ways; not so much giving of presents, or sending of cards, as postage was dear then. The cost of living was high too, and only the rich could afford any feasting. The condition of our poor was bad. The disastrous effect of the Union upon trade and commerce was bitterly felt, and poverty stalked where once had been plenty. But the well-off citizens tried to forget all that. They feasted well, and drank plenty of punch. There was dancing too. The waltz had become popular, and young people everywhere were dancing to the beautiful music of a young Austrian composer with the name of Johann Strauss.

Dublin Historical Record, 1943

from OWENEEN THE SPRAT

E. OE. Somerville & Martin Ross

I was labouring in the slough of Christmas letters and bills, when my wife came in and asked me if I would take her to the Workhouse.

'My dear,' I replied, ponderously, but, I think, excusably, 'you have, as usual, anticipated my intention, but I think we can hold out until after Christmas.'

Philippa declined to pay the jest the respect to which its age entitled it, and replied inconsequently that I knew perfectly well that she could not drive the outside car with the children and the Christmas tree. I assented.

Philippa's Workhouse Tea took place on Christmas Eve. We were still hurrying through an early luncheon when the nodding crest of the Christmas tree passed the dining-room windows. My youngest son immediately upset his pudding into his lap; and Philippa hustled forth to put on her hat, an operation which, like the making of an omelette, can apparently only be successfully performed at the last moment. With feelings of mingled apprehension and relief I saw the party drive from the door, the Christmas tree seated on one side of the car, Philippa on the other, clutching her offspring, Denis on the box, embosomed, like a wood-pigeon, in the boughs of the spruce fir. I congratulated myself that the Quaker, now white with the snows of many winters, was in the shafts. Had I not been too deeply engaged in so arranging the rug that it should not trail in the mud all the way to Skebawn, I might have noticed that the lamps had been forgotten.

It was, as I have said, Christmas Eve, and as the afternoon wore on I began to reflect upon what the road from Skebawn would be in another hour, full of drunken people, and, what was worse, of carts steered by drunken people. I had assured Philippa (with what I believe she described as masculine *esprit de corps*) of Denis's adequacy as a driver, but that did not alter the fact that in the last rays of the setting sun I got out my bicycle and set forth for the Workhouse. When I reached the town it was dark, but the Christmas shoppers showed no tendency to curtail their operations on that account, and the streets were filled with an intricate and variously moving tide of people and carts. The paraffin lamps in the shops did their best, behind bunches of holly, oranges, and monstrous Christmas candles, and partially illumined the press of dark-cloaked women and more or less drunken men, who swayed and shoved and held vast conversations on the narrow pavements. The red glare of the chemist's globe transformed the leading female beggar of the town into a being from the Brocken; her usual Christmas family, contributed for the festival by the neighbours, as to a Christmas number, were grouped in fortunate ghastliness in the green light. She

extracted from me her recognised tribute, and pursued by her assurance that she would forgive me now till Easter (i.e. that further alms would not be exacted for at least a fortnight), I made my way onward into the outer darkness, beyond the uttermost link in the chain of public-houses.

The road that led to the Workhouse led also to the railway station; a quarter of a mile away the green light of a signal post stood high in the darkness, like an emerald. As I neared the Workhouse I recognised the deliberate footfall of the Quaker, and presently his long pale face entered the circle illuminated by my bicycle lamp. My family were not at all moved by my solicitude for their safety, but, being in want of an audience, were pleased to suggest that I should drive home with them. The road was disgustingly muddy; I tied my bicycle to the back of the car with the rope that is found in wells of all outside cars. It was not till I had put out the bicycle lamp that I noticed that the car lamps had been forgotten, but Denis, true to the convention of his tribe, asseverated that he could see better without lights. I took the place vacated by the Christmas tree, the Quaker pounded on at his usual stone-breaking trot, and my offspring, in strenuous and entangled duet, declaimed to me the events of the afternoon.

It was without voice or warning that a row of men was materialised out of the darkness, under the Quaker's nose; they fell away to right and left, but one, as if stupefied, held on his way in the middle of the road. It is not easy to divert the Quaker from his course; we swung to the right, but the wing of the car, on my side, struck the man full in the chest. He fell as instantly and solidly as if he were a stone pillar, and, like a stone, he lay in the mud. Loud and inebriate howls rose from the others, and, as if in answer, came a long and distant shriek from an incoming train. Upon this, without bestowing an instant's further heed to their fallen comrade, the party took to their heels and ran to the station. It was all done in a dozen seconds; by the time the Quaker was pulled up we were alone with our victim, and Denis was hoarsely suggesting to me that it would be better to drive away at once. I have often since then regretted that I did not take his advice.

89

The victim was a very small man; Denis and I dragged him to the side of the road, and propped him up against the wall. He was of an alarming limpness, but there was a something reassuring in the reek of whisky that arose as I leaned over him, trying to diagnose his injuries by the aid of a succession of lighted matches. His head lay crookedly on his chest; he breathed heavily, but peacefully, and his limbs seemed uninjured. Denis, at my elbow, did not cease to assure me, tremulously, that there was nothing ailed the man, that he was a stranger, and that it would be as good for us to go home. Philippa, on the car, strove as best she might with the unappeasable curiosity of her sons and with the pig-headed anxiety of the Quaker to get home to his dinner. At this juncture a voice, fifty yards away in the darkness, uplifted itself in song: 'Heaven's refle-hex! Killa-ar-ney!' it bawled hideously.

It fell as balm upon my ear, in its assurance of the proximity of Slipper.

'Sure I know the man well,' he said, shielding the flame of a match in his hand with practised skill. 'Wake-up, me *bouchaleen*!' He shook him unmercifully. 'Open your eyes, darlin'!'

The invalid here showed signs of animation by uttering an incoherent but, as it seemed, a threatening roar. It lifted Denis as a feather is lifted by a wind, and wafted him to the Quaker's head, where he remained in strict attention to his duties. It also lifted Philippa.

'Is he very bad, do you think?' she murmured at my elbow. 'Shall I drive for the doctor?'

'Arrah, what docthor?' said Slipper magnificently. 'Give me a half a crown, Major, and I'll get him what meddyceen will answer him as good as any docthor! Lave him to me!' He shook him again. 'I'll regulate him!'

The victim here sat up, and shouted something about going home. He was undoubtedly very drunk. It seemed to me that Slipper's ministrations would be more suitable to the situation than mine, certainly than Philippa's. I administered the solatium; then I placed Denis on the box of the car with the bicycle lamp in his hand, and drove my family home. . .

Further Experiences of an Irish RM, 1908

PREPARATIONS FOR THE CHRISTMAS PARTY

Brian Moore

'The streamers,' said Miss Albee, 'should stretch from each corner of the ceiling and join in the centre. Then we'll put the paper bell at the centre join.'

'And the mistletoe?' Mrs Clapper asked. 'Will it hang on the bell?'

Gavin, holding one end of the paper streamer, winked at Freddy, who was holding the other. 'That wouldn't do,' Freddy said solemnly.

'And why not?' Miss Albee wanted to know.

'Because how could we kiss under the mistletoe? The table would be in the way.'

'Oh,' said Miss Albee. She looked down at the paper bell, twiddling it in her hands. Freddy and Gavin affixed the streamer and put the mistletoe over the door. Wee Bates came in with paper and pencil. 'Soldier says I'm to lift five bob off everybody for the party.'

'But I'm teetotal,' Miss Albee objected.

'It's two bob for teetotals,' Wee Bates said. 'We'll have orange crush and ginger ale for them as wants it.'

Miss Albee and Mrs Clapper went to get their purses. Freddy and Gavin paid and their names were entered on Wee Bates' sheet. Soldier MacBride and Jimmy Lynan arrived, carrying a large cardboard box. 'Gather round,' Soldier said. 'Wait'll you see this.' He began to unpack the box, revealing paper hats, favors, a big fruitcake, a plum pudding, several bags of toffee, and some oranges. 'Courtesy of the Ladies' Red Cross Auxiliary,' Soldier said. 'I went around there this afternoon. Comforts for the troops.'

'But why should they give them to us?' Miss Albee asked. 'We're not the Forces.'

'And are we any different from some young conscript sitting in front of an anti-aircraft gun in Lurgan?' Soldier wanted to know. 'Aren't we in the front line of Home Defence?'

Miss Albee, who was Loyal Ulster and who knitted socks for the soldiers, shook her head, disapprovingly. 'I'd hardly say that. I think it's a disgrace, giving comforts to the likes of us.'

'Maybe so, maybe so,' said Soldier. He began to repack his box. Your Man Mick Gallagher came in from the yard, carrying a scuttle full of coal.

91

'Five bob for drinks for the party,' Wee Bates said, holding out his hand. Your Man stared at Bates, then unbuttoned his battle-dress jacket and showed a tiny Sacred Heart button pinned to his undershirt. 'This, here,' he said, looking at Soldier, not at Bates, 'do you know what this is?'

'Indeed I do,' Soldier said. 'The Pioneer Total Abstinence Association, a grand organisation, founded by Father Mathew, RIP. Ireland sober is Ireland free.'

'Correct.'

'Right then,' Soldier said. 'Just pay two bob for minerals.'

'But I don't want no minerals. I don't want no party.'

'Get away with you,' Soldier said, jovially. 'Sure, Christmas comes but once a year.'

'Aye, and I'll have my Christmas dinner at home. Not with outsiders.'

'But we'll all have our dinners at home,' Soldier said. 'This is just a bit of jollification on the premises. And how can you call us outsiders, us that's been cooped up in this wee house together, day in and day out for a whole long year?'

'Youse are still outsiders to me,' said Your Man.

At that moment, Post Officer Craig entered the room, followed by Old Crutt, his stoolie. Wee Bates, sheet in hand, went up to them. 'Collecting for the party, sir. Five bob for the drinks, please?'

'What drinks?' Craig said.

'Christmas Day, sir.'

'Minerals only. I said, minerals only.'

Soldier looked at Freddy, who looked at Gavin, who looked at Jimmy Lynan. It was as though they passed the remark around to make sure it had really been uttered. 'Minerals, of course, for them that wants them,' Soldier said. 'And a few dozen of stout and a bottle of whisky for the rest of us. Right, Mr Craig, sir?'

'You heard me the first time, MacBride.'

'But surely to God. It's Christmas Day.'

'Minerals only.'

'But even in the trenches, sir, in the last war, I remember –'

'I don't care what you remember.'

'It's allowed in the other posts,' Freddy said. 'In Post 204, for instance.'

'What Post 204 does is Post 204's business. What this post does is my business. No drinking on duty.'

'Ah, it's that business of the Captain,' Soldier said. 'Ah, I don't blame you one bit, Mr Craig. But we're a cut above the Captain, sir. We're sensible men.'

'I've had enough trouble,' Craig said, darkly. 'None of youse knows the trouble I've had.'

'Ah, but a few stout, sir –'

'No. There's a war on. I said, there's a war on.'

There was a long moment of silence. Craig moved over to Miss Albee and Mrs Clapper. 'Well, ladies, and how is the decorations coming along?'

'Rightly, Mr Craig.'

'That's good. I want to see a good turnout of decorations. Something nice, and in keeping.'

'Yes, Mr Craig.'

'Right, then. Carry on.'

He left the room. The men turned and looked at Old Crutt, the stoolie. Old Crutt, comprehending, followed in his master's footsteps.

'That man,' Soldier said, 'is not Christian. Eh, Jimmy?'

Look at Lynan, said the Black Angel. *That* man is ready to kill. Remember the pub. It was no joke, that threat. No joke, no matter what Sally says.

Lynan, breathing heavily, turned toward Freddy. 'One brick,' he whispered. 'One brick, right between he's eyes.'

Uneasily, Freddy nodded. Soldier, smiling, took the paper bell from Miss Albee and pinned it at the centre join of the streamers. Big Frank Price came in from the front office. 'Yellow warning,' he said.

'Not again.' There were groans. In the past month there had been three yellow, or preliminary, warnings, followed by siren alerts. Nothing had happened. It was a sour joke around Belfast that the sirens were sounded at night to wake the ARP personnel from their slumbers. After the second false warning, few citizens bothered to go down to the shelters, for now, reading about the mounting count of raids on Britain, everyone knew that the Germans had decided to ignore Northern Ireland. So, when the sirens wailed, people turned over in their beds. Usually, the all clear was sounded within fifteen minutes.

The sirens sounded shortly after Big Frank's announcement. Ten minutes later, the all clear was given. Freddy and Gavin, on their way upstairs to play ping-pong, met Your Man Gallagher coming down from the attic. He was wearing his steel helmet and carrying his gas mask rucksack. 'Bloody Germans,' he muttered. 'Bloody Germans.'

The Emperor of Ice Cream, 1966

WHITE CHRISTMAS

W.R. Rodgers

Punctually at Christmas the soft plush
Of sentiment snows down, embosoms all
The sharp and pointed shapes of venom, shawls
The hills and hides the shocking holes of this
Uneven world of want and wealth, cushions
With cosy wish like cotton-wool the cool
Arm's-length interstices of caste and class,
And into obese folds subtracts from sight
All truculent acts, bleeding the world white.

Punctually that glib pair, Peace and Goodwill,
Emerge royally to take the air,
Collect the bows, assimilate the smiles,
Of waiting men. It is a genial time.
Angels, like stalactites, descend from heaven,
Bishops distribute their own weight in words,
Congratulate the poor on Christlike lack,
And the member for the constituency
Feeds the five thousand, and his plenty back.

Punctually to-night, in old stone circles
Of set reunion, families stiffly sit
And listen; this is the night, and this the happy time
When the tinned milk of human kindness is
Upheld and holed by radio-appeal.

Hushed are hurrying heels on hard roads,
And every parlour's a pink pond of light
To the cold and travelling man going by
In the dark, without a bark or a bite.

But punctually to-morrow you will see
All this silent and dissembling world
Of silted sentiment suddenly melt
Into mush and watery welter of words
Beneath the warm and moving traffic of
Feet and actual fact. Over the stark plain
The stilted mill-chimneys once again spread
Their sackcloth and ashes, a flowing mane
Of repentance for the false day that's fled.

Awake! and other poems, 1941

THE HEADLESS RIDER OF CASTLE SHEELA

James Reynolds

Christmas Day at Castle Sheela was far from a merry one. All day long
there was a tension in the air that affected all within the house. Countess
Höja's neuralgia assailed her, so she kept to her room. Caro and Brigid
tried embroidery. No use. Late in the morning they took the terriers for a
walk through the old rabbit warrens at the back of the paddock. This
kept the girls busy until they returned to join Dominic for a late lunch.
Dominic had spent the morning browsing among his father's books in
the library. 'Too cold to hunt,' he said.

In Terrance and Brendan Mallory's day, Christmas dinner at Castle
Sheela had been a meal in the great tradition. On this particular
Christmas, dinner was set for six o'clock in the evening, with Ormond
Mallory presiding at the head of his table.

The day dragged on. Six o'clock came, but no Ormond appeared.
Everyone knew the hunt had found its last fox around four o'clock.
Dominic had walked out to the gate house and talked with the hunts-
men returning to Clonboy Castle. They told Dominic they had had a
good day.

Mary Corty, the cook, was frantic. Dinner had been ready and waiting
to be served these two hours. 'It'll be a great ruin, and meself destroyed
with the labour,' she moaned. Then Kirstey, the maid who had opened
the door early that morning for Follow, heard a noise on the stone steps
of the entrance porch. It sounded like a heavy body stumbling. Then
came the whinnying of a horse, a sobbing kind of whinnying, that of a
horse far spent in wind. Kirstey ran to the door and flung it wide open.
At the same moment Dominic appeared in the door of the library.

A foundering horse stumbled across the threshold of the hall door.
His russet hide was streaked and matted with dried blood and lather.
Astride his back rode horror, the very definition of horror – the body of a
man, the legs tied with rope under the horse's belly, the wrists tied
together behind the back. The dark green coat with silver buttons was
torn and saturated with blood. Above the collar of this coat there was no
head. Ormond Mallory's head had been severed cleanly from his body.

Too stunned by the shock of what they saw to move, Kirstey and
Dominic sank back against the wall. Follow, his sides heaving in his last
effort, slowly mounted the runway, as he had done daily for years. At
the door of his master's bedroom he sank to the floor, dead.

The head of Ormond Mallory was never found, nor was his murderer
ever discovered. Jason Fermoy, the neighbouring landowner who had
met Ormond in the lane and beaten him with a shillelagh, as Jason later
told at the Assizes Court, fell under suspicion and was interrogated by

Mr Justice Callahan. Jason proved, beyond doubt, a watertight alibi. He was dismissed. A curious annotation on the margin of this phase of the case is that, for years after the murder, Mrs Fermoy, heavily veiled, visited the grave of Ormond Mallory in the churchyard at Clonboy. After one of her visits a piece of paper, which she had tucked into a metal flower vase, was disturbed by an errant wind. The paper blew along one of the cemetery paths and was picked up by a lay priest who happened to be passing. Written in heavy black ink on a piece of stiff white paper was this:

EPITAPH

HE WAS WICKED, DESPERATELY WICKED.
BUT HE INVESTED WICKEDNESS
WITH A BRIGHTNESS AND SPARKLE
WHICH MADE IT EXCEEDINGLY ATTRACTIVE.

Ghosts in Irish Houses, 1947

PEACE AND GOODWILL TO MANAGERS

George Bernard Shaw

The Babes in the Wood The Children's Grand Pantomime.
By Arthur Sturgess and Arthur Collins. Music by J.M. Glover, Theatre Royal, Drury
Lane, 27 December 1897.

I am sorry to have to introduce the subject of Christmas in these articles.
It is an indecent subject; a cruel, gluttonous subject; a drunken, disorderly subject; a wasteful, disastrous subject; a wicked, cadging, lying,
filthy, blasphemous, and demoralizing subject. Christmas is forced on a
reluctant and disgusted nation by the shopkeepers and the press: on its
own merits it would wither and shrivel in the fiery breath of universal
hatred; and anyone who looked back to it would be turned into a pillar of
greasy sausages. Yet, though it is over now for a year, and I can go out
without positively elbowing my way through groves of carcases, I am
dragged back to it, with my soul full of loathing, by the pantomime.

The pantomime ought to be a redeeming feature of Christmas, since it
professedly aims at developing the artistic possibilities of our Saturnalia.
But its professions are like all the other Christmas professions: what the
pantomime actually does is to abuse the Christmas toleration of
dullness, senselessness, vulgarity, and extravagance to a degree utterly
incredible by people who have never been inside a theatre. The manager
spends five hundred pounds to produce two penn'orth of effect. As a
shilling's worth is needed to fill the gallery, he has to spend three
thousand pounds for the 'gods', seven thousand five hundred for the
pit, and so on in proportion, except that when it comes to the stalls and
boxes he caters for the children alone, depending on their credulity to
pass off his twopence as a five-shilling piece. And yet even this is not
done systematically and intelligently. The wildest superfluity and extravagance in one direction is wasted by the most sordid niggardliness in
another. The rough rule is to spend money recklessly on whatever can
be seen and heard and recognized as costly, and to economize on
invention, fancy, dramatic faculty – in short, on brains. It is only when
the brains get thrown in gratuitously through the accident of some of the
contracting parties happening to possess them – a contingency which
managerial care cannot always avert – that the entertainment acquires
sufficient form or purpose to make it humanly apprehensible. To the
mind's eye and ear the modern pantomime, as purveyed by the late Sir
Augustus Harris, is neither visible nor audible. It is a glittering, noisy
void, horribly wearisome and enervating, like all performances which
worry the physical senses without any recreative appeal to the emotions
and through them to the intellect.

Our Theatres in the Nineties, 1898

MERRY CHRISTMAS, 1778

Sir Jonah Barrington

Close to the kennel of his hounds my father had built a small cottage, which was occupied solely by an old huntsman, his older wife, and his nephew, a whipper-in. The chase, and the bottle, and the piper were the enjoyments of winter, and nothing could recompense a suspension of these enjoyments.

My elder brother justly apprehending that the frost and snow of Christmas might probably prevent their usual occupation of the chase, determined to provide against any listlessness during the shut-up period by an uninterrupted match of what was called 'hard-going' till the weather should break up.

A hogshead of superior claret was, therefore, sent to the cottage of old Quin, the huntsman; and a fat cow, killed and plundered of her skin, was hung up by the heels. All the windows were closed to keep out the light. One room, filled with straw and numerous blankets, was destined for a bed-chamber in common, and another was prepared as a kitchen for the use of the servants. Claret, cold, mulled, or buttered, was to be the beverage for the whole company, and in addition to the cow above mentioned, chickens, bacon and bread were the only admitted viands. Wallace and Hosey, my father's and brother's pipers, and Boyle, a blind but a famous fiddler, were employed to enliven the banquet, which it was determined should continue till the cow became a skeleton, and the claret should be on its stoop.

My two elder brothers; two gentlemen of the name of Taylor, one of them afterwards a writer in India; a Mr Barrington Lodge, a rough songster; Frank Skelton, a jester and a butt; Jemmy Moffat, the most knowing sportsman of the neighbourhood; and two other sporting gentlemen of the county, composed the permanent bacchanalians. A few visitors were occasionally admitted.

As for myself, I was too unseasoned to go through more than the first ordeal, which was on a frosty St Stephen's Day, when the 'hard-goers' partook of their opening banquet, and several neighbours were invited, to honour the commencement of what they called their 'shut-up pilgrimage'.

The old huntsman was the only male attendant, and his ancient spouse, once a kitchen-maid in the family, now somewhat resembling the amiable Leonarda in Gil Blas, was the cook, whilst the drudgery fell to the lot of the whipper-in. A long knife was prepared to cut collops from the cow; a large turf fire seemed to court the gridiron; the pot bubbled up as if proud of its contents, whilst plump white chickens floated in crowds upon the surface of the water; the simmering potatoes,

Seajan · macCaemaoil · del.

just bursting their drab surtouts, exposed the delicate whiteness of their mealy bosoms; the claret was tapped, and the long earthen wide-mouthed pitchers stood gaping under the impatient cock, to receive their portions. The pipers plied their chants, the fiddler tuned his Cremona, and never did any feast commence with more auspicous appearances of hilarity and dissipation, appearances which were not doomed to be falsified.

I shall never forget the attraction this novelty had for my youthful mind. All thoughts but those of good cheer were for the time totally obliterated. A few curses were, it is true, requisite to spur on old Leonarda's skill, but at length the banquet entered: the luscious smoked bacon, bedded in its cabbage mattress, and partly obscured by its own savoury steam, might have tempted the most fastidious of epicures; whilst the round trussed chickens, ranked by the half dozen on hot pewter dishes, turned up their white plump merry-thoughts, exciting equally the eye and appetite; fat collops of the hanging cow, sliced indiscriminately from her tenderest points, grilled over the clear embers upon a shining gridiron, half-drowned in their own luscious juices, and garnished with little pyramids of congenial shallots, smoked at the bottom of the well-furnished board. A prologue of cherry-bounce (brandy) preceded the entertainment, which was enlivened by hob-nobs and joyous toasts.

Numerous toasts, in fact, as was customary in those days, intervened to prolong and give zest to the repast – every man shouted forth his fair favourite, or convivial pledge; and each voluntarily surrendered a portion of his own reason in bumpers to the beauty of his neighbour's toast. The pipers jerked from their bags appropriate planxties to every jolly sentiment; the jokers cracked the usual jests and ribaldry; one songster chanted the joys of wine and women; another gave, in full glee, the pleasures of the fox chase; the fiddler sawed his merriest jigs; the old huntsman sounded his horn, and thrusting his forefingers into his ear, to aid the quaver, gave the 'view halloa!' of nearly ten minutes' duration, to which melody 'tally ho!' was responded by every stentorian voice. A fox's brush stuck into a candlestick, in the centre of the tables, was worshipped as a divinity! Claret flowed, bumpers were multiplied, and chickens, in the garb of spicy spitchcocks, assumed the name of devils to

99

whet the appetites which it was impossible to conquer!

My reason gradually began to lighten me of its burden, and in its last efforts kindly suggested the straw-chamber as my asylum. Two couple of favourite hounds had been introduced to share in the joyous pastime of their friends and master; and the deep bass of their throats, excited by the shrillness of the huntsman's tenor, harmonised by two rattling pipers, a jiggling fiddler, and twelve voices, in twelve different keys, all bellowing on one continuous unrelenting chime, was the last point of recognition which bacchus permitted me to exercise, for my eyes began to perceive a much larger company than the room actually contained; the lights were more than doubled, without any virtual increase of their number, and even the chairs and tables commenced dancing a series of minuets before me. A faint tally ho! was attempted by my reluctant lips; but I believe the effort was unsuccessful, and I very soon lost, in the straw-room, all that brilliant consciousness of existence in the possession of which the morning had found me so happy.

Just as I was closing my eyes to a twelve hours' slumber, I distinguished the general roar of 'stole away!' which rose almost up to the very roof of old Quin's cottage.

At noon, next day, a scene of a different nature was exhibited. I found, on waking, two associates by my side, in as perfect insensibility as that from which I had just aroused. Our piper seemed indubitably dead! But the fiddler, who had the privilege of age and blindness, had taken a hearty nap, and seemed as much alive as ever.

The room of banquet had been re-arranged by the old woman; spitchcocked chickens, fried rashers, and broiled marrow-bones appeared struggling for precedence. The clean cloth looked itself fresh and exciting; jugs of mulled and buttered claret foamed hot upon the refurnished table, and a better or heartier breakfast I never in my life enjoyed.

A few members of the jovial crew had remained all night at their posts, but, I suppose, alternately took some rest, as they seemed not at all affected by their repletion. Soap and hot water restored at once their spirits and their persons; and it was determined that the rooms should be ventilated and cleaned out for a cock-fight, to pass time till the approach of dinner.

In this battle-royal every man backed his own bird, twelve of which courageous animals were set down together to fight it out, the survivor to gain all. In point of principle, the battle of the Horatii and Curiatii was reacted, and in about an hour one cock crowed out his triumph over the mangled body of his last opponent, being himself, strange to say, but little wounded. The other eleven lay dead, and to the victor was unanimously voted a writ of ease, with sole monarchy over the hen-roost for the remainder of his days; and I remember him for many years the proud commandant of his poultry-yard and seraglio. Fresh visitors were introduced each successive day, and the seventh morning had arisen before the feast broke up. As that day advanced, the cow was proclaimed to have furnished her full quantum of good dishes; the claret was upon its stoop, and the last gallon, mulled with a pound of spices, was drunk in tumblers to the next merry meeting! All now retired to their natural rest, until the evening announced a different scene.

An early supper, to be partaken of by all the young folks of both sexes in the neighbourhood, was provided in the dwelling-house to terminate the festivities. A dance, as usual, wound up the entertainment, and what was then termed a 'raking pot of tea' put a finishing stroke, in jollity and good humour, to such a revel as I never saw before, and, I am sure, shall never see again.

Personal Sketches of his own Times, 1827–32

DEPRESSION CHRISTMAS

W.J. Johnston

Corner of Bellevue Street: December night,
The dirty slush is gleaming in the dark,
A gusty wind makes all the gas lamps flicker,
Christmas is in the windows. Lights from shops
Shine on the pavement and the slanting sleet,
And on the passing faces, an out-of-work
Stands gazing, hands in pockets, meagre frame
Slumped in his clothes, cap over hopeless eyes;
Woman beside him, puny child in arms,
A thin shawl drawn round both. Expressionless,
They gaze with dull eyes apathetically,
'All that you need for home we can supply'
So runs the sign, but they stand motionless,
The sleet slants down upon them. The child cries,
The woman shivers and moves on. The man
His baggy trousers holed about the knee
And frayed about the ankle, stands in light
A moment, and goes after aimlessly,
The night hides both.
Yes, everything for home – behind glass windows!

Poems of a Parachute Padre, 1943

THE MAGI

W.B. Yeats

Now as at all times I can see in the mind's eye,
In their stiff, painted clothes, the pale unsatisfied ones
Appear and disappear in the blue depth of the sky
With all their ancient faces like rain-beaten stones,
And all their helms of silver hovering side by side,
And all their eyes still fixed, hoping to find once more,
Being by Calvary's turbulence unsatisfied,
The uncontrollable mystery on the bestial floor.

Later Poems, 1922

CHRISTMAS PARTIES AND PAPER HATS

J.D. Sheridan

Almost every periodical that runs to a Christmas Number (and the only ones that don't are the telephone directory and the Summer Bus Guide) gets a member of the staff to dig up and modernize, or has foisted on it by an outside contributor, that traditional standby of the Double Number, *Hints for Your Christmas Party*. And for the life of me I can't see why. For except in prisons, big hotels, and the sergeants' mess, there is no such thing as a Christmas party. The Christmas party was invented by Dickens, and eagerly adopted by modern writers of crime stories, who have to have some excuse for getting a herd of suspects together under one roof.

I resent the suggestion that one cannot face Christmas properly without a collection of puzzles, games, and mathematical posers. I regard it as an affront to the tradition of near-gluttony and indolence that marks Christmas in respectable middle-class homes that can't afford it.

But the most degrading feature of these unnecessary hints for non-existent parties is the batch of illustrations that goes with it. The main idea in the artist's mind is that a person in a paper hat is necessarily enjoying himself: which is a gross exaggeration. A young man in a paper hat that leaves his curls showing may be enjoying himself, and a young girl in a paper hat that suits her (which is the only kind of paper hat that a young girl will wear) is almost certainly enjoying herself. But a middle-aged man in a paper hat that makes him look repulsive (which is the only kind of paper hat made) is already comatose – if he weren't, he wouldn't permit this indignity to his face.

At the paper-hat stage of the Christmas dinner I can pull a cracker as well, or as badly, as any man of my age. I pull with the ponderous insensibility of an elephant dragging a log out of a swamp. I pull without hilarity, almost without emotion. And I know what is coming. The other party to the contract may get a hat that will show off his curls, or be kind to the tilt of her nose, but I am doomed from the start. I get a hat that splits on my skull and makes me look like Crippen, Jack the Ripper, or the Last Days of Henry the Eighth.

But I don't care. At that stage of the Christmas dinner I am past caring. I am replete. I am as relaxed as an ox after a long day in deep pasture. If you took a photograph of me and my paper hat you could give it any title you like – from 'Freak Potato' to 'Curious Cloud Formation on Mount Everest'.

A middle-aged man in a Christmas paper hat is fit only to move from the table, evict his eldest son from the armchair, and reflect on the annual problem of how to doze off without either letting his cigar go out or setting fire to his paper hat. He grunts when he is offered fruit, grunts when he is asked to put coal on the fire, grunts when someone suggests a cup of tea, and grunts when the children run across his toes.

But – and make no mistake about it – he is not bored. His spirit is not broken. He is still head of the house. He is a very Christian gentleman, taking his rest and enjoying himself in the great old European tradition. He may seem half asleep; he may seem wholly asleep; but he is still in control of his faculties.

And you can prove it by asking him to join in any of the imbecilities of the magazine-type Christmas party – to take two matches from twelve and leave thirteen, or get a penny from under a tumbler without touching the tumbler, or choose any card from the pack. He may be wearing a paper hat, he may be looking like a fried egg, but he is not to be trifled with.

Admittedly, he won't answer you in words, for he is beyond words. But he will answer you. He will rise from his chair in slow instalments, look at you like a wounded lion from beneath the eaves of his torn paper hat, and go majestically upstairs to bed.

My Hat Blew Off, 1950

MOCK GOOSE – A DAINTY DISH FOR YULETIDE

Anon

This is a splendid Christmas dish for the economical housekeeper, who cannot invest in a feathered creature of any description. Buy four pounds of steak, and make it tender by beating and rubbing with lemon juice. After sewing up the steak to make a kind of carcase, fill it with a nice sage and onion stuffing. Roast this on Christmas Day, together with sausages, and serve with sauces and vegetables just as though it were roast goose.

Henderson's Quarterly Magazine, 1910

The McCooeys

BELFAST'S RADIO FAMILY CREATED BY JOSEPH TOMELTY

NO 6.
McCooey's Christmas Party

This week with being so busy in the shop I haven't had much time to find out what has been going on at the McCooey's. I know Maggie got word she would be getting out of hospital a couple of days before Christmas and with getting things ready Sarah has been complaining about having to spend most of her time in town buying Maggie's presents.

With Sally taking a notion of the young doctor she hasn't been about the house much and Meta has had to set to and get things in order for her mother coming home.

Oul Granda is in great form and he's just after shouting in on his way to the market. He's always on the look-out for a bargain

'I'M GLAD TO SEE YR MA HOME META. I'M JUST NOT CUT OUT FOR LOOKING AFTER A GROWN-UP FAMILY. SURE I'M THAT TIRED THESE NIGHTS THAT I'VE GOT TO TAKE A PILL TO GET ME ASLEEP. IT'S A GOOD JOB CHRISTMAS ONLY COMES ONCE A YEAR!'

'YOUR RIGHT THERE AUNT SARAH. ALL THIS WORK IS JUST RUININ' MY HANDS. IT WOULDN'T BE SO BAD IF SALLY HAD GIVEN US A PULL OUT BUT SHE'S BEEN 'GALLIVANTIN' AROUND ALL WEEK WITH THIS 'DOCTOR KILDARE FELLA. HE'S TURNED HER HEAD IF YOU ASK ME. I SUPPOSE SHE'LL BE BRINGING HIM ALONG TO THE PARTY— IF HE'S NOT TOO HIGH AND MIGHTY TO COME!'

'THERE'S AN OLD MILL BY THE STREAM NELLIE DEAN'

'HERE IT IS SARAH A BIRD FIT FOR A KING. A REAL TURKEY DELIGHT THE MAN THAT SOLD US IT SAYS ITS BREST WILL BE AS WHITE AS THE 'DRIVEN SNOW''

'THAT'S A LOVELY DROP OF WINE BOBBY'

'THIS IS SOME HOMECOMING. IT'S THE BEST PARTY THE MCCOOEYS HAVE EVER HAD. YOU KNOW BOBBY 'YR A SHOCKIN' MAN. YOU SHOULD'NT HAVE BROUGHT ALL THAT WINE IN, YOU KNOW WE'RE NOT USED TO IT. THE WHIFF OF A CORK IS ENOUGH TO SET SARAH OFF.'

'HERE MAGGIE HAVE A CIGARETTE.' NOW DON'T BE ANGRY WITH ME. Y... Y... KNOW I'M NOT ONE FOR THE BOTTLE BUT CHRISTMAS IS A SPECIAL OCCASION AND IT'S A HOMECOMING TOO. THAT'S ONE OF THEM NEW WINES THAT YOU SEE ADVERTISED ON THE TELE. I'L SAY ONE THING FOR IT MAGGIE IT MAKES YR TOES OPEN AND SHUT'

'I'M NOT SURE I AGREE WITH ALL THIS DRINKING GRANDA. YON BOBBY GREER'S NOT FIT TO BITE HIS THUMB. WHAT WILL SALLY'S YOUNG MAN THINK ABOUT US. BOBBY'S BEEN AT HIM ALL NIGHT TO GET HIM TO EXAMINE HIS CHEST. SURE THE OUL' FOOL SHOULD KNOW ITS ONLY THE WIND THAT'S WRONG WITH HIM. HE TOOK THAT SECOND HELPING OF PLUM PUDDIN' TOO QUICK. I'LL HAVE A WORD TO SAY TO HIM WHEN HE'S SOBER!'

'WOULD YOU LOOK AT OUL' GRANDA HE'S ABOUT DUE TO GIVE US 'DANNY BOY' ANY MINUTE'

'NOW SARAH WHERE'S YOUR CHRISTMAS FEELING—GOODWILL TOWARDS ALL MEN . YOU KNOW SALLY'S TAKEN QUITE A SHINE TO THAT YOUNG DOCTOR. HE'S A WEE BIT TOO 'MALONE ROAD FOR ME. STRIKES ME AS BEING A WEE BIT TOO GOOD TO BE TRUE. YOU KNOW SOME OF THESE MEDICAL FELLAS SAY MORE THAN THEIR PRAYERS. I HOPE HE'S SERIOUS ABOUT IT — FOR SALLY'S SAKE'

NEXT WEEK—
SALLY'S BIG ROMANCE

THE WREN-BOY

Brendan Kennelly

The little eagle-conquering wren has died
For him, tautly poised on the threshold there,
Gaunt in his fomorian pride;
White feathers in his hair,
Swaddled in gold and green,
His right fist flicks the swarthy stick
And beats the goatskin tambourine.

The majesty of Stephen's Day
Is on his face, grown proud as Lucifer
As he begins to play;
Lithe bodies stir
To his music, cries
Of praise unfold and
Fierce pride leaps in his eyes.

As the ancient drumbeat rings
From beaten skin, he steps
Into the days of unremembered kings;
Alone, he tops
This day of hectic moments in a flood
Of notes, their gay swashbuckling passion
Crashing through his blood.

Christmas townlands wait,
Carrig, Lenamore,
Road and field, they undulate
To every open door;
Village, byre and frosty ways
Show farmer, townie, whining crone
Grow generous with praise.

He knows dominion now
And leaves behind
The heavy spade, the ponderous plough
For glory in the mind
And blood; a man whose pride
In stick and drum commemorates
The bird that died.

Good Souls to Survive. 1967

FATHER'S CHRISTMAS PARTY

Sam McAughtry

Now when I was a young man, I was, of all the family, the one who spent most time in Dad's company when he was at home. This is not because I had any more special relationship than the other brothers had with him: no, it was because the brothers had things to do outside of drinking pints, and I hadn't, and when Dad was at home he became unsettled and nervous if he had to sit around the house for any length of time. 'Throw on your coat and come on,' he would say to me in the mornings, and in the afternoons and in the evenings. 'Where are we going?' I would ask. 'We'll take a bit of a dander and get the fresh air,' he would say. About a minute and a half later the two of us would discover, to our surprise, that we had landed up outside Jimmy McGrane's pub in Spamount Street. and in we would go, to get out of the cold. It was only to be expected therefore that Dad's second Christmas at home should leave its mark on me, more so than anybody else.

It was 1950, a year before I was married, and a year before Dad died and was buried in Cuba. There were just the three brothers, the sister and myself at home, for Mother was four years dead then. Father's ship tied up in Immingham in Yorkshire a week before Christmas, and he wasn't due to sail until the 27th. 'Right Sam,' he said, the minute he hit Belfast off the Liverpool boat, 'you and me have to stock up for the Christmas party.' 'Where are we having it?' I asked. 'In the parlour,' he said. We called in for a jar on the way home from the boat, and when I left I was humping a dozen of stout, the first of the special party stock. After the sister had coaxed him into eating a wee pick of fried ham and a cup of milky tea. round to Jimmy McGrane's we went: 'I'm going to be home for Christmas,' Dad said to all his cronies, 'and I'm throwing a party.'

At first I wrote down the names of the acceptors, but no paper could have held out to it. 'We're going to need some drink for *this* party,' I told him. 'Right ther.,' he said, 'go up to the bar and get some,' and with that he thrust a handful of mint-fresh notes at me. On the 22nd, 23rd and 24th of December our parlour began to look more and more like Jimmy McGrane's. There was drink everywhere. The sister wasn't too sure what to do about it all. For all our lives we'd been used to Dad just going round for a mouthful, and coming back like a gentleman, but well under control for all that – and now things seemed to be heading for an unmerciful binge, and in the parlour too, a place reserved for the clergyman, or maybe the insurance man, if he was paying out on a policy.

'Do the parlour up a bit,' Dad said, 'make it look like a bar.' So I put a lick of paint on it, and rigged up a makeshift bar out of a sideboard and a china cabinet, covered with curtain material.

'Right,' I said to Dad on Christmas Eve morning, 'the bar's all ready, we've enough drink for the First Battalion of the Rifles: what time does the party start?'

'Midnight,' he said. I gaped at him. 'Well,' says he, 'the pubs'll be open till ten, and we usually bring a carry-out, don't we? So it'll be midnight before we finish our normal drinking. I've told the guests to arrive at twelve, and to prepare for an all-night session.' 'How old are you now?' I asked him. 'Sixty-eight,' he said. 'Excuse me asking,' I said, 'but what did your mother feed you on?' 'I don't see what you're driving at,' he said, and so help me God he didn't.

They came from far and near to Dad's Christmas party, and every blessed guest brought a bottle. Standing behind the bar, I tried desperately to get them to take the drink we'd left in, but the stock actually grew larger as the morning wore on. I heard Dad reminisce with old pals he hadn't seen for years upon years. 'Do you mind the time we rolled the hundredweight of cheese down the gangway at one in the morning?' one old seadog said. 'Aye, I do,' Dad said, 'that was in Cork. We sold it to a publican for a bottle of whiskey.'

It was a lovely party: a delightful party. They were standing on top of each other, singing songs, and weeping and shaking hands. When it finally came to an end at dawn, seven or eight of the guests had to be carried and laid out on sofas or beds. And Dad was as steady as a rock. And as happy as he could be without my mother.

On Boxing Night I left him down to the Liverpool boat. 'What on earth am I going to do with all that liquor in the parlour?' I asked him as we shook hands.

'What do you usually do with liquor?' he asked. 'You drink it, don't you?'

And away he went to sea, at sixty-eight years of age. Five feet four, and seven stone ten. The quart into a pint pot champion of the world.

Sam McAughtry's Belfast, 1981

CHRISTMAS CONVERSION

Alexander Irvine

About the first of November, each year, there was a falling in attendance at the Sunday School of the Parish Church, and a corresponding increase in the Sunday School of the Methodists in the Kill Entry. Each year we were warned. Each year we turned a deaf ear to the warning. We were not deserters or 'turncoats'. Our annual lapse was not due to disloyalty. The Methodists used to give a Christmas Soiree. Hot coffee and buns were served, with an address by an escaped missionary as a sort of spiritual salad. The Methodists knew all about our needs and capacities. They were generous to a fault, and we denizens of the alleys just took advantage of the buns they annually cast upon the turgid waters of the underworld.

About the first of January we slunk back again and rehabilitated ourselves. I presume we were catalogued in both organisations as 'floating population'. But that hot coffee and the buns were worth all the disgrace they cost.

Souls of Poor Folk, 1921

THE FRENCH INVASION OF BANTRY BAY, 1796

Theobald Wolfe Tone

December 25th. These memorandums are a strange mixture. Sometimes I am in preposterously high spirits, and at other times I am as dejected, according to the posture of our affairs. Last night I had the strongest expectations that today we should debark, but at two this morning I was awakened by the wind. I rose immediately, and, wrapping myself in my greatcoat, walked for an hour in the gallery, devoured by the most gloomy reflections. The wind continues right ahead, so that it is absolutely impossible to work up to the landing-place, and God knows when it will change. Had we been able to land the first day and march directly to Cork, we should have infallibly carried it by a *coup de main,* and then we should have a footing in the country; but as it is – if we are taken, my fate will not be a mild one; the best I can expect is to be shot as an *emigre rentre,* unless I have the good fortune to be killed in the action; for most assuredly if the enemy will have us he must fight for us. Perhaps I may be reserved for a trial, for the sake of striking terror into others, in which case I shall be hanged as a traitor, and embowelled, etc. As to the embowelling, *Je m'en fiche';* if ever they hang me, they are welcome to embowel me if they please. These are pleasant prospects! Nothing on earth could sustain me now but the consciousness that I am engaged in a just and righteous cause. For my family, I have by a desperate effort, surmounted my natural feelings so far, that I do not think of them at this moment. This day, at twelve, the wind blows a gale, still from the east, and our situation is now as critical as possible; for it is morally certain that this day or to-morrow on the morning the English fleet will be in the harbour's mouth, and then adieu to everything. In this desperate state of affairs I proposed to Cherin to sally out with all our forces to mount the Shannon, and, disembarking the troops, make a forced march to Limerick, which is probably unguarded, the garrison being, I am pretty certain, on its march to oppose us here; to pass the river at Limerick, and, by forced marches, push to the North. I detailed all this on a paper which I shall keep, and showed it to Captain Bedout and all the generals on board – Chérin, Simon, and Chasseloup. They all agreed as to the advantages of the plan, but after settling it we find it impossible to communicate with the General and Admiral, who are in the *Immortalité,* nearly two leagues ahead, and the wind is now so high and foul, and the sea so rough, that no boat can live, so all communication is impracticable, and tomorrow morning it will, most probably, be too late; and on this circumstance perhaps the fate of the expedition and the liberty of Ireland depends. I see nothing before me, unless a miracle be wrought in our favour, but the ruin of the expedition,

the slavery of my country, and my own destruction. Well, if I am to fall, at least I will sell my life as dear as individual resistance can make it. So now I have made up my mind. I have a merry Christmas of it, today.

Autobiography of Theobald Wolfe Tone, 1893

from FATHER CHRISTMAS

Michael McLaverty

'Will you do what I ask you?' his wife said again, wiping the crumbs off the newspaper which served as a tablecloth. 'Wear your hard hat and you'll get the job.'

He didn't answer her or raise his head. He was seated on the dilapidated sofa lacing his boots, and behind him tumbled two of his children, each chewing a crust of bread. His wife paused, a hand on her hip. She glanced at the sleety rain falling into the backyard, turned round, and threw the crumbs into the fire.

'You'll wear it, John – won't you?'

Again he didn't answer though his mind was already made up. He strode into the scullery and while he washed himself she took an overcoat from a nail behind the kitchen door, brushed it vigorously, gouging out the specks of dirt with the nose of the brush. She put it over the back of a chair and went upstairs for his hard hat.

'I'm a holy show in that article,' he said, when she was handing him the hat and helping him into the overcoat. 'I'll be a nice ornament among the other applicants! I wish you'd leave me alone!'

'You look respectable anyhow. I could take a fancy for you all over again,' and she kissed him playfully on the side of the cheek.

'If I don't get the job you needn't blame me. I've done all you asked – every mortal thing.'

'You'll get it all right – never you fear. I know what I'm talking about.'

He hurried out of the street in case some of the neighbours would ask him if he were going to a funeral, and when he had taken his place in the line of young men who were all applying for the job of Father Christmas in the Big Store he was still conscious of the bowler hat perched on top of his head. He was a timid little man and he tried to crouch closer to the wall and make himself inconspicuous amongst that group of grey-capped men. The rain continued to fall as they waited for the door to open and he watched the drops clinging to the peaks of their caps, swelling and falling to the ground.

'If he had a beard we could all go home,' he heard someone say, and he felt his ears reddening, aware that the remark was cast at him. But later when he was following the Manager up the brass-lipped stairs, after he had got the job, he dwelt on the wisdom of his wife and knew that the hat had endowed him with an air of shabby respectability.

'Are you married?' the Manager had asked him, looking at the nervous way he turned the hat in his hand. 'And have you any children?' He had answered everything with a meek smile and the Manager told him to stand aside until he had interviewed, as a matter of form, the rest of the applicants.

And then the interviews were quickly over, and when the Manager and John were mounting the stairs he saw a piece of caramel paper sticking to the Manager's heel. Down a long aisle they passed with rows of counters at each side and shoppers gathered round them. And though it was daylight outside, the electric lights were lit, and through the glare there arose a buzz of talk, the rattle of money, and the warm smell of new clothes and perfume and confectionery – all of it entering John's mind in a confused and dreamy fashion for his eye was fastened on the caramel paper as he followed respectfully after the Manager. Presently they emerged on a short flight of stairs where a notice – PRIVATE – on trestles straddled across it. The Manager lifted it ostentatiously to the side, ushered John forward with a sweep of his arm, and replaced the notice with mechanical importance.

'Just a minute,' said John, and he plucked the caramel paper from the Manager's heel, crumpled it between his fingers, and put it in his pocket.

They entered the quiet seclusion of a small room that had a choking smell of dust and cardboard boxes. The Manager mounted a stepladder, and taking a large box from the top shelf looked at something written on the side, slapped the dust off it against his knee, and broke the string.

'Here,' he said, throwing down the box. 'You'll get a red cloak in that and a white beard.' He sat on the top rung of the ladder and held a false face on the tip of his finger: 'Somehow I don't think you'll need this. You'll do as you are. Just put on the beard and whiskers.'

'Whatever you say,' smiled John, for he always tried to please people.

Another box fell at his feet: 'You'll get a pair of top boots in that!' The Manager folded the step-ladder, and daintily picking pieces of fluff from his sleeves he outlined John's duties for the day and emphasised that after closing-time he'd have to make up parcels for the following day's sale.

Left alone John breathed freely, took off his overcoat and hung it at the back of the door, and for some reason whenever he crossed the floor he did so on his tiptoes. He lifted the red cloak that was trimmed with fur, held it in his outstretched arms to admire it, and squeezed the life out of a moth that was struggling in one of the folds. Chips of tinsel glinted on the shoulders of the cloak and he was ready to flick them off when he decided it was more Christmassy-looking to let them remain on. He pulled on the cloak, crossed on tiptoes to a looking-glass on the wall and winked and grimaced at himself, sometimes putting up the collar of the cloak to enjoy the warm touch of the fur on the back of his neck. He attached the beard and the whiskers, spitting out one or two hairs that had strayed into his mouth.

'The very I-T,' he said, and caught the beard in his fist and waggled it at his reflection in the mirror. 'Hello, Santa!' he smiled and thought of his children and how they would laugh to see him togged up in this regalia. 'I must tell her to bring them down some day,' and he gave a twirl on his toes, making a heap of paper rustle in the corner.

He took off his boots, looked reflectively at the broken sole of each and pressed his thumb into the wet leather: 'Pasteboard – nothing else!' he said in disgust, and threw them on the heap of brown paper. He reached for the top boots that were trimmed with fur. They looked a bit on the small side. With some difficulty he squeezed his feet into them. He walked across the floor, examining the boots at each step; they were very tight for him, but he wasn't one to complain, and, after all, the job was only for the Christmas season and they'd be sure to stretch with the wearing.

When he was fully dressed he made his way down the stairs, lifted his leg over the trestle with the name PRIVATE and presented himself on one of the busy floors. A shop-girl, hesitating before striking the cash-register, smiled over at him. His face burned. Then a little girl plucked her mother's skirt and called, 'Oh, Mammy, there's Daddy Christmas!' With his hands in his wide sleeves he stood in a state of nervous perplexity till the shop-girl, scratching her head with the tip of her pencil, shounted jauntily: 'First Floor, Santa Claus, right on down the stairs!' He stumbled on the stairs because of the tight boots and when he halted to regain his composure he felt the blood hammering in his temples and he wished now that he hadn't listened to his wife and worn his hard hat. She was always nagging at him, night, noon and morning, and he doing his damned best!

On the first floor the Manager beckoned him to a miniature house – a house painted in imitation brick, snow on the eaves, a door which he could enter by stooping low, and a chimney large enough to contain his head and shoulders, and inside the house stacks of boxes neatly piled, some in blue paper and others in pink.

The Manager produced a hand-bell. 'You stand here,' said the Manager, placing himself at the door of the house. 'Ring your bell a few times – like this. Then shout in a loud, commanding voice: "Roll up now! Blue for the Boys, and Pink for the Girls."' And he explained that when business was slack, he was to mount the ladder, descend the chimney, and bring up the parcels in that manner, but if there was a crowd he was just to open the door and shake hands with each child before presenting the boxes. They were all the same price – a shilling each.

For the first ten minutes or so John's voice was weak and self-conscious and the Manager, standing a short distance away, ordered him to raise his voice a little louder: 'You must attract attention – that's what you're paid for. Try it once again.'

114

'Blue for the Boys, and Pink for the Girls!' shouted John, and he imagined all the buyers at the neighbouring counters had paused to listen to him. 'Blue for the Boys, and Pink for the Girls!' he repeated, his eye on the Manager who was judging him from a distance. The Manager smiled his approval and then shook an imaginary bell in the air. John suddenly remembered about the bell in his hand and he shook it vigorously, but a shop-girl tightened up her face at him and he folded his fingers over the skirt of the bell in order to muffle the sound. He gained more confidence, but as his nervousness decreased he became aware of the tight boots imprisoning his feet, and occasionally he would disappear into his little house and catching the sole of each in turn he would stretch them across his knee.

But the children gave him no peace, and with his head held genially to the side, if the Manager were watching him, he would smile broadly and listen with affected interest to each child's demand.

'Please, Santa Claus, bring me a tricycle at Christmas and a doll's pram for Angela.'

'I'll do that! Everything you want,' said Father Christmas expansively, and he patted the little boy on the head with gentle dignity before handing him a blue parcel. But when he raised his eyes to the boy's mother she froze him with a look.

'I didn't think you would have any tricycles this year,' she said. 'I thought you were only making wooden trains.'

'Oh, yes! No, yes. Not all all! Yes, of course, I'll get you a nice wooden train.' Father Christmas turned to the boy in his confusion. 'If you keep good I'll have a lovely train for you.'

'I don't want an oul train, I want a tricycle,' the boy whimpered, clutching his blue-papered parcel.

'I couldn't make any tricycles this year,' consoled Father Christmas. 'My reindeers was sick and three of them died on me.'

The boy's mother smiled and took him by the hand. 'Now, pet, didn't I tell you Santa had no tricycles? You better shout up the chimney for something else – a nice game or a wooden train.'

'I don't want an oul game – I want a tricycle,' he cried, and jigged his feet.

'You'll get a warm ear if you're not careful. Come on now and none of your nonsense. And Daddy Christmas after giving you a nice box, all for yourself.'

Forcibly she led the boy away and John, standing with his hands in his sleeves, felt the prickles of sweat on his forehead and resolved to promise nothing to the children until he had got the cue from the parents. . .

Collected Short Stories, 1978

115

from UPON A DYING LADY

W.B. Yeats

VII

Her Friends bring her a Christmas Tree

Pardon, great enemy,
Without an angry thought
We've carried in our tree,
And here and there have bought
Till all the boughs are gay,
And she may look from the bed
On pretty things that may
Please a fantastic head.
Give her a little grace,
What if a laughing eye
Have looked into your face?
It is about to die.

Collected Poems, 1950

CHRISTMAS AMONG THE PEASANTRY

William Carleton

Christmas Day passed among the peasantry as it usually passes in Ireland. Friends met before dinner in their own, in their neighbours', in shebeen or in public houses, where they drank, sang, or fought, according to their natural dispositions, or the quantity of liquor they had taken. The festivity of the day might be known by the unusual reek of smoke that danced from each chimney, by the number of persons who crowded the roads, by their brand-new dresses – for if a young man or country girl can afford a dress at all, they provide it for Christmas – and by the striking appearance of those who, having drunk a little too much, were staggering home in the purest happiness, singing, stopping their friends, shaking hands with them or kissing them, without any regard to sex. Many a time might be seen two Irishmen, who had got drunk together, leaving a fair or market, their arms about each other's necks, from whence they only removed them to kiss and hug one another the more lovingly. Notwithstanding this, there is nothing more probable than that these identical two will enjoy the luxury of a mutual battle, by way of episode, and again proceed on their way, kissing and hugging as if nothing had happened to interrupt their friendship. All the usual effects of jollity and violence, fun and fighting, love and liquor, were, of course, to be seen, felt, heard, and understood on this day, in a manner much more remarkable than on common occasions; for it may be observed that the national festivals of the Irish bring out their strongest points of character with peculiar distinctness.

The Midnight Mass, 1833

TURKEY AND HAM

Lynn Doyle

When wee Mr Anthony the solicitor was courtin' Mr Livingston's daughter, Miss Betty, he had only the one trouble. It wasn't his girl; she was a quiet simple affectionate slip of a grey-eyed girl, an' thought the sun riz an' set on him. The bother was, Mr Anthony was so pleased about it that he begun to put on fat. He told me his trouble, one day we were out shootin' over the Bermingham estate, that Miss Betty's father was agent for; an' I only laughed at him.

'What odds does it make,' says I, 'if your young lady takes no notice.'

That comforted him for a while; but the followin' week a thunderbolt fell on him.

'George,' sez Miss Betty to him one evenin', very timid, 'I'm thinkin' of tryin' to slim. It would never do for the two of us to get fat,' sez she. 'People would look after us as we sent down the street.'

Mr Anthony jumped as if he had touched an electric wire.

'That settles it,' sez he. 'I needed that jog. Not that I'm greedy, dear; but I'm a great judge of food and wine, and it seemed a pity not to exercise my talent. Now, my mind is made up. As from the end of to-night's dinner – I'll have to eat that, since it's cooked – I go on a diet till I've lost a stone and a half. I will not have you slimming, Betty. Curse it,' says he, 'I don't care if you grow as round as a dumpling. I love you. But we mustn't become ridiculous. Listen to me, darling,' he says, warmin' up; 'from to-night I go on to Dr Thompson's diet. It's a corker, mind you. It slimmed old Mrs McGimpsey till she rattled in her coffin; and it may kill me, too; but my word is my oath. Damme, if it wasn't boiled chicken and bacon I'd give to-night's dinner to the dog.'

'Don't overdo it, George,' sez Miss Betty, a trifle frightened. 'You might injure your health. And you forget that to-morrow's Christmas

Day, and you're dining with us.'

'I was doing more than that,' sez Mr Anthony. 'I was dining in the middle of the day as well, just to spite my old housekeeper. She has my Christmas dinner bought, a turkey and a ham, and sausages and chestnuts and heaven knows what; and I got a present of two bottles of champagne from Mr Bermingham – the Widow Clicquot, 1921 – that would make a tombstone angel play jazz tunes.'

'But George, darling,' says Miss Betty, 'were you going to eat and drink all that? And I was sympathizing about your figure!'

'Confound it, no,' says Mr Anthony. 'I never get anything but a morsel, a couple of slices of breast, and maybe a wing and a sausage or two; and then off goes the rest to her relations. She has a sister married to the gamekeeper of the Bermingham estate, and another to the keeper of the back lodge-gate, and you'd think she was married to them herself. They get about two-thirds of all the food I pay for; and now they're going to get the whole of my Christmas dinner.'

'But it's a shame,' says Miss Betty, 'an imposition!'

Mr Anthony stopped on the road.

''Gad,' says he, 'I never thought of that. It *is* an imposition. I've been weak, Betty,' sez he, 'and that's not like me. I can't eat my Christmas dinner – grape-fruit and toast, the doctor's diet says – and I can't drink my Christmas champagne; but, begad, if I fast the housekeeper's relatives may fast too, Pat Murphy's coming round this evening after dinner to fix up some shooting for St. Stephen's Day. I'll give my dinner to him. Not a word!' says he. 'I want to show you that you're getting a man that loves you better than his meals. It's a point of honour with me, now. Damme,' sez he, 'I'll stick to the diet should I go up the aisle with you, and the people looking through me as if I was a rainbow.'

The Ballygullion Bus. 1957

NATIVITY

James Simmons

Milton reckoned the snow's motive was right
to hide from God the foulness of the earth,
to please the father make the son's first night
a cold one, the mother's a hard birth.

A daft conceit, but true. The white lies
of respectability always trouble the poor,
weeding their diction of deformities,
jostling the cripple, the wino, the hooer.

The mayor wants to worship God, but turns
his children away from the front door,
while in his hearth a tame inferno burns,
gift of Prometheus, workman and welcomer.

Judy Garland and the Cold War, 1976

A MERRY CHRISTMAS

Tomás O'Crohan

It was the morning of Christmas Eve. 'I fancy that I may as well go and get a sheep,' said I to my mother.

'Don't go,' says she. 'Give windy Diarmid his chance. We shall find out whether he comes up to his trumpeting. If he kills that big sheep there'll be enough for the two houses in her, but I'm afraid he won't make good his swaggering.'

She had far less confidence in him than I had. I expected that he'd keep his promise, if he did lay the big sheep low. He was a finished butcher, for those brothers had a big household when they kept house together. And often enough had the joker put a knife in a fine sheep of their flock without anybody telling him to.

I strolled out late in the evening to look if the cows were coming down from the hill, and what should I see but the rascal coming to the house with half the big sheep on his back. Diarmid had split the sheep so cleanly in two that half the head was still sticking to half the body.

When he went in, he threw off his load.

'There's a joint for you, little woman, for the Holy Day,' says he.

'May this day a year hence find you and us all in prosperity and joy,' said she.

Just at that moment in I came. I looked at the present.

'Yerra, a blessing on your arms, good old uncle!' said I. 'You're a man of your word if anybody is.'

'Didn't I tell you that I'd do it?' said he. 'Sure, if it hadn't been for you and the help of God, I shouldn't have been alive to kill it. It's in honour of God that I killed it, and to share it with you. I shall never forget the seals' cave!'

I turned away from him and went to the box. I took out one of the four bottles that remained there, and came up to him.

'There, you've earned this drink to-day if you ever did, Diarmid.'

'Mary Mother! wherever did you get it all?' says he.

'Didn't you get a bottle from your friends yourself?'

'Devil a one except one my old friend Muirisin Bán gave me.'

Well, I filled him a glass and a half, for that was the full of the vessel I held in my hand.

'O, King of the Angels! don't you know that my old skeleton can't take in all that at one gulp after the day's toil?'

'This is the little Christmas drink.'

He seized the glass, and before long all its contents were in a place that kept them safe, and he said directly:

'I hope with God that we shall have a good Christmas and a good

Shrove to follow.'

Then he jumped up and ran out through the door.

I ran after him and brought him in again.

'Yerra, aren't you in a hurry?' said I.

'O!' says he, 'to-night isn't like other nights, and it isn't right for me to fail my own little crowd on God's Blessed Eve.'

I'd always thought that he wasn't so devout as he showed himself that day, for he was always a rough-tongued chap, and it was his constant habit to go seeking help from hell whenever he was in a rage. His expressions that day increased the respect I had for him. After a bit he went off.

When the time for lighting up came on 'God's Blessed Eve,' if you were coming towards the village from the south-east – for that's the direction in which every door and window faces – and every kind of light is ablaze that night, you would imagine it a wing of some heavenly mansion, though it is set in the middle of the great sea. You would hear a noise in every house that night, for, however much or little drink comes to the Island, it is put aside for Christmas Eve. Maybe an old man would be singing who'd never lifted his voice for a year. As for the old women, they're always lilting away.

I felt that I would rather go out a bit than spend the whole evening at home. The place I meant to go to was Pat Heamish's house for a bit, for he wasn't too well yet. I knew that he hadn't got a drop of drink, so I got a half-pint. There was a score or so of welcomes waiting for me. He was a man you could get a great deal of sport out of, but he was anything but happy, as he hadn't got a drop for Christmas. He'd drunk up all that he'd brought with him from Dingle, as his health had gone to pieces after the carouse.

I handed him the half-pint.

'Drink that down,' said I to him, 'for you've got to sing a song.'

'You'll get no song,' says Kate, 'if he once gets the half-pint down.'

'I'll sing a song, too,' says Tom.

He drank a tot and sang, not one song, but seven of them.

On Christmas Day and during the Christmas season we used to have hurley matches, and the whole village used to be mixed up in the game. Two men were chosen, one from each side, for captains. Each of them would call up man by man in turn until all who were on the strand were distributed in the two sides. We had hurleys and a ball. The game was played on the White Strand without shoes or stockings, and we went in up to our necks whenever the ball went into the sea. Throughout the twelve days of Christmas time there wasn't a man able to drive his cow to the hill for the stiffness in his back and his bones; a pair or so would have a bruised foot, and another would be limping on one leg for a month.

That Christmas Day my two uncles, Diarmid and Tom, were on opposite sides. I was on Diarmid's side, and that's where I preferred to be, for, if I had chanced to be against him, I couldn't have put out half my strength if I had been anywhere near him.

We won three games from them, one after another, and the two sides were raging – they struggling to win one game, anyhow, in the day and the other side swaggering.

When we were approaching the cliff path on our way home, 'O, shame on you!' says uncle Diarmid, 'we didn't let you win a single game since morning.'

When Diarmid made that remark, his brother Tom was going up the path, just in front of him. He turned down, and raising his fist, gave him a blow in the ear-hole that sent him down on to the strand a cold corpse or nearly.

'Sure, you little devil, it wasn't you that did it.'

He hadn't far to fall, but it was rough ground. He lost his speech, for it was knocked clean out of him, and it was an hour before he could talk, with all the others about him on the strand, all except the man who hit him – he'd gone home. Before long his feeble voice began to strengthen, and when it came back he made no good use of it, for the first thing he said was: 'On my body and soul, I swear I'll be the priest at that fellow's deathbed!'

They set him on his feet, and he wasn't long in coming to himself. He only had a scratch or two on his cheek. We went off home, and it was as much as we could do, we were so tired after the day.

The Islandman, 1937
(translated by Robin Flower, 1951)

CHRISTMAS ON REMAND

Brendan Behan

I met Charlie in the recess, and we wished each other a 'happy Christmas'.

All the blokes wished each other a 'happy Christmas', quiet-like so as the screws wouldn't hear them talking; it would not do to go too far on Christmas morning.

We banged out our doors and washed ourselves, waiting for the breakfast being brought up.

When they came to my door, I heard one of them saying that I was an RC and would not be getting my breakfast till after church service. This was on account of most of the RCs going to Communion, and I was going to say out through the spy-hole that I was not going and was to get my breakfast in the usual way, when I heard the screw saying to the orderly that I was not allowed to go to anything like that and that I was getting my breakfast with the rest.

He opened my door and asked, 'You're not for Communion are you?'

'No, sir,' said I.

'Well, 'ere's your breakfast then!' He was a nice old bloke for that morning anyway and added, 'Anyway, Paddy, you get your scoff now and don't 'ave to wait an hour and 'alf for it.'

I took it from him and thanked him and he banged out the door. I always like breakfasts and I always like mornings, and the old screw trying to be nice to me had put me in good humour.

When we RCs fell in for Mass, the boy beside me whispered that we would see Dale that morning. Be God and so we will, said I to myself, sitting up with the chokey blokes in front, and I heard the boys saying along the line that he would be there to be seen and we'd see how the chokey was affecting him.

We marched out of the wing and had to cross a yard but the snow was glittering white in the sunshine and the sky was blue.

We went in our seats and sat down while the rest of the chapel filled up. At the back of us were old men and younger ones, doing every sort of sentence from seven days to fifteen years, and they all kind of smiled at each other, for it being Christmas.

When all the other seats were filled up and five or six hundred men in the chapel, the chokey merchants were marched into the very front seats and separated from the ones behind them by an empty row. They were all on either Number One, bread and water; or Number Two, bread and water with porridge and potatoes at midday. They had been in chokey, some of them, for five months, and some of them had not been out of the punishment cells to Mass during that time. They seemed to appreciate

124

being brought out today, and looked neither to right nor left as they came in but sat right down and looked straight ahead at the altar.

All the prisoners looked white by comparison with the screws, but these prisoners from chokey were Persil white by comparison with the other prisoners.

The YPs gave each other tiny nudges when we picked out Dale amongst the other prisoners from chokey. He seemed to have forgotten us, or how he'd sat back in the seat previous Sundays, and just looked straight in front like the others from chokey.

The priest came out and the chokey prisoners were the first and quickest on their knees. We all got down to it, and knelt till the sermon, when we stood for the gospel and sat down to listen to the priest.

He started off telling us that the greeting was not peace and goodwill to men on earth, but peace on earth to men of goodwill, and went on to say that Christmas was a time of prayer as well as a time for enjoying yourself.

'It is not for us, as it is for thoughtless people outside the church, or for those who have forgotten the very significance of Christ's Mass, just a time for feasting, a mere Bank Holiday. True, we rejoice, as Christians should, at the birth of our Divine Lord, and welcome Him, with the gifts of a good confession and communion, as did the Three Kings of the East. I mean they welcomed Him with gifts, too. Not with the Sacraments, which were yet to be instituted, but with gifts. I use the word in its symbolic sense. And while not as the lantern-jawed Calvinist, that tried to eradicate from this England of ours the very memory of the feast, that generation of gloom, as the great Chesterton called them. Himself, Chesterton, a great man in all senses of the word, a fat man, jolly in God, as sound a judge of beer as he was of theology. We make rejoicing, and think with love all the time even as we break the crackling of the goose, even as we savour the tender white meat of the turkey.'

The chokey merchants in the front seats never took their eyes off the priest, and he looked kindly back at us all, and went on with the sermon.

'As we pour the sauce over that homely symbol of our own dear Christian land, the plum pudding, heavy, dark, rich and laden rarely with fruits of sunnier climes, Spain usually, and Italy, and while we enjoy the wine, as Christians should for, as I think it was Belloc remarked, it was given us in the first miracle, and liqueurs are to this day made by Carthusians, Dominicans, Benedictines and if I may mention, in this our own dear land, at Buckfast, the monks make a good wine, but,' here he smiled and we smiled with him, 'in accordance with what I suppose is the traditionally more austere tradition of this, called by William Shakespeare, whom, as you know, lived and died in the Old Faith, "sceptered isle" for medicinal purposes only. Or as we pour ourselves a foaming glass of ale, and draw on our cigar –'

The prisoners drew their breath in unison with the preacher, and some of the fellows on punishment swallowed and rubbed their mouths with the backs of their hands.

'– we do so, remembering the great love God bore us, love that brought down this day to Mary ever blessed Virgin, conceived without sin, and to Joseph, her most chaste spouse, a little child to die for our salvation on a wooden cross, nailed and crucified to show His love for us.'

He looked serious here and we looked serious with him.

'Love as deep as the deepest ocean, as wide as the farthest horizon. Many of you have been mariners and you know how wide that is.'

We all looked round, and the screws did too at prisoners nodding in agreement all over the chapel, even some of the chokey prisoners nodded. They didn't nod to the rest of us, but only to each other, who had been mariners, and up at the priest, who nodded back, and went on with the sermon.

'A tender love, a forgiving love, the love of a father for his children, the love of brother for brother, and in that spirit and in that love, to those of you who are of goodwill, I wish a holy and happy Christmas.'

The organ struck up a hymn, then, and we all joined in:

> See amid the winter's snow,
> Born for us, on earth below,
> See the tender Lamb appear,
> Promised from eternal year.

The chokey merchants left the chapel first, filing out of the door, looking neither right nor left, for their morning bread and water. The rest of us waited until they were gone and then we went back to our wings.

It was still very cold and the snow heavy on the ground but bright and clean to look at, just for the minute we were marching across the yard to our wing.

We got our smoking exercise in the end of the wing away from the others. There had been rumours that everyone was getting five Woodbines to smoke that day, the convicted and all, but when the convicted saw us remands and awaiting trials being called away to smoke separate from them they knew that they were getting no smoke.

I walked round behind Charlie, and we smiled at each other, and when he got a chance to whisper he said that maybe next month we'd have been weighed off at the Assizes and be in Borstal.

Well, we had the Assizes to look forward to. It was a big day out, sometimes a couple of days, if your case went on, or if you were not called the first day, and you got tea and bully sandwiches. Sometimes they made a kind of a pasty made with the bully and it was called Sessions Pie.

126

Yes. I smiled a bit and whispered to Charlie that from this good day it would be getting better, instead of worse, and we could smell the dinner coming up, and it smelt great.

It was as good as its smell. Usually the screws shouted out, 'Bang out your doors' the minute we took the diet can off the tray, but this day I took my diet can into the cell, put it on the table, and banged out the door.

In the top shallow tier of the can were three lovely golden-brown roasted potatoes with chopped green vegetable and in the long part was roast meat, a piece of Yorkshire pudding, at least that's what I thought it was, and gravy, and all roasting hot with steam running in pearls down the side of the can.

I was looking at it with delight and already had it eaten with my eyes when the screw came back to the cell.

'Don't you want your duff?'

He turned to someone else on the landing outside and said, 'Paddy, 'ere, 'e doesn't want 'is duff,' and went to walk off.

'I do, I do,' I shouted, and hoping to Christ he would not go off.

But he'd only been joking, and opened the door. It was the old Cockney, and there was a great smell of beer off him. He smiled as he handed me my duff and poured custard on it from a ladle.

'There you are, Paddy. That'll put 'air on your chest. We was forgetting all about you, we was.' He smiled again and nodded to the orderly to take up the tray and can of custard.

'A happy Christmas to you, sir,' said I, on an impulse of liking.

He looked at me for a second and then said, 'And the same to you, son and many of 'em.'

I banged out the door and got out the dinner on the plate. It lay hot and lovely, the roast potatoes, the Yorkshire pudding, the chopped greens and the meat, and a big piece of bread to pack up with, and it wasn't long before I had it finished, and the plate clean (not that I left anything on it) for the duff and custard.

And then the door opened again and the screw gave me the *News of the World*. I'd forgotten that the day before was Sunday. He just threw it in the cell to me, and banged out the door again.

Ah, better again, said I to myself, opening the paper, this is making a good day yet.

But after I heard the bells of the city strike three I knew we were not getting any more exercise, and I put down the paper to save a bit of a read for the night. It was getting too dark to read anyway, so I put down the paper and thought I'd walk up and down for a bit. But it was so cold that I didn't want to take off my shoes, so I just sat there crouched up on the chair leaning on the table, hugging into myself to get a bit of heat.

They brought round the supper about a quarter to four and it warmed me up for a while, and I decided I'd go to bed, for they'd hardly come round now till eight o'clock. I lay in bed after I'd eaten my supper and drunk my cocoa, and was warm, anyway.

I thought of home and my family sitting round the fire in Dublin, where there were forty hearths that would welcome me but, to tell the truth, I only thought of them because I thought it was what I should do, in my situation; and it was only for a moment I went on thinking of them, and then I came back here to my cell in the cold, and at least they had put the light on at tea-time so I had another read of the *News of the World,* but the light was in my eyes, and it was cold on my arms outside the blankets, so I put the paper down, and my hands inside the bed-clothes, and must have fallen asleep, for the next thing I remember was doors opening and being banged out and prisoners shouting.

Jesus, they must be making all the fellows get up till eight o'clock, I thought, and that maybe the bastards would report me to the Governor if I was caught in bed. The screw whoever he was was coming nearer and, by Christ, the fellows were getting very defiant all of a sudden, shouting and cursing: 'Fugh off, you rotten bastard'. . . 'Fugh off. . .'

Jesus, what was happening? I struggled, standing on the cold slate floor, to get my shorts on. I'd never get the bed up in time. But if the others were ballocking the screw, I'd be as good as the rest anyway.

Charlie's door I heard being banged, and he shouting, 'Arn. . . you bastard. . .' and then my own door opened.

Christ, what's this? A small, rat-faced screw, never said yes, aye, or no about the bed being made down or anything else, but he handed me an envelope and looked at me, with little nervous eyes, and banged out the door and went on to the next cell.

I opened the envelope and found in it a card. It was not personally addressed to me but to 'a prisoner', and wished me a happy and holy Christmas and blessings in the New Year from the General of the Salvation Army.

'Ah, you bastard,' I shouted after the screw, 'stuff you and him,' just in time to hear the next fellow let a roar and a string of curses after the screw, while he went on his rounds delivering his greetings.

Nearly every cell that he threw a card into he got shouts and curses from it in return, a thing I had never heard in Walton before, but sweet Jesus, the dirty little bastard, was it coming to make a jeer of us altogether he was?

I put the General's Christmas card convenient to where I'd be using it in the morning and got back into bed again.

For there was no reason to believe that that screw would be coming back to get us out of bed, barring he was coming back to case us all for the Governor in the morning, so fugh him and his happy Christmas. I'd have committed a sin with myself, only I was too indignant to get my mind concentrated, so I just lay in bed and fell asleep again.

The next day, Stephen's Day, or Boxing Day as they called it here, we had no church services but, in compensation I suppose, we had work in the afternoon, and went down and sewed mailbags in the hall together, till four o'clock just as any other day. So we went into our cells that night and ate our supper and drank our cocoa, glad to know that this bloody Christmas lark was over, and next day an ordinary day, with blokes going up and down to court and all.

Borstal Boy, 1958

THE POOR LITTLE CLERK WHO'D NEVER GOT A CHRISTMAS CARD BEFORE

Paul Yates

Sweet
guy, almost *wet himself* getting it open
there
he was swinging round in his office chair
sticking his thumb
under
the flap ripping it open
not seeing the wire
and then
just as he was about to read the message

BANG

Sky made of Stone, 1976

CHRISTMAS WAYFARERS

Cathal O'Byrne

Redden the hearth and sweep the floor,
let the candle-light through the pane be showing,
bring sweet well water, and leave the door
loose on the hasp, for who would be knowing
what poor soul, lonely and travelled far,
walking the world on the naked highway
might follow the gleam of the Candle Star,
and its welcome win in this lonesome byeway.

So, for sake of two who went out from the city
by bridle lanes down to Bethlehem
and who failed to find there, for love or pity,
a kindly soul who would welcome them,
redden the hearth, let the comfort-sharing
glow of the peat-fire shine fair and bright,
and may a tired, poor Man and a Maiden wearing
a mantle of blue, be our guests to-night.

Christmas Wayfarers, 1932

AMUSEMENTS FOR CHRISTMAS PARTIES

Anon

Sometimes even at Christmas parties an uncomfortable pause, a lull in the flow of social merriment, occurs. Uncle, when requested to tell a ghost story, puffs contemplatively at his cigar, and says that it is too early; besides, the children would be frightened by his harrowing narrative. Aunt Jane, too, is obviously tired of accompanying all and sundry on the drawing room piano, and no one exactly knows how to profitably occupy the two hours' interval before supper is announced. As a matter of fact, everyone is weary of the routine of song, story, and recitation, and the psychological moment has arrived for the introduction of the amusing sports similar to those we illustrate.

Five minutes devoted to the following game, which is really a feat of balancing, will do more to create roars of laughter than any number of comic songs.

A broomstick is placed through the handles of an ordinary tin bath or clothes basket, and rested upon two chairs, so that the utensil swings freely. Four pennies are now placed on the backs of the chairs, one on each of the corners, and the preparations are complete.

Anyone who considers himself an expert balancer is now at liberty to seat himself in the bath, and with the aid of a walking-stick knock off the four coins from the corners of the chairs, and step to the ground again.

To everyone's surprise, directly this is attempted, the bath appears to become animated with the properties of a bucking horse, and in nine cases out of ten whoever attempts to knock off the coins is thrown to the ground amidst shrieks of laughter.

'Matching-burning races' are very amusing. Any number of people can engage in them, and the prize goes to the one whose match burns longest. The secret of winning a match race is to keep the burning match steadily revolving in an upright position.

'Japanese fights' are great fun. Two competitors enter for the contest. They are blindfolded, and lay down on the floor at full length, each holding the left hand of the other and carrying in their free hands a long roll of paper to act as a weapon. The rules of the contest are as follows: Each combatant must lie at full length, the left hands must be clasped, and it is only allowable to rise up on the knees when delivering a blow. The difficulty of striking one's opponent with the paper bludgeon is extraordinary, and the spectacle of two men squirming on the floor and cautiously stalking and prospecting and delivering mighty blows amidst the applause of the onlookers, is one of the most ludicrous imaginable.

One of the most difficult feats to perform and which will cause much amusement is to pick up a newspaper from the floor with the mouth. Not one person out of a hundred can perform this exploit without releasing the hold on the foot and thereby breaking the rules of the game.

A very laughable game is the one played with a chair and a pin. The pin is inserted in the side of the chair originally, and the game is to withdraw the pin with the mouth and then replace it. This requires some expertness, as at the slightest shifting of balance the chair is liable to overturn, to the discomfiture of the performer and to the enjoyment of the spectators. A variation of this game is to extract sixpence from beneath the leg of a chair; but in all cases the position shown in the photograph must be adhered to.

'Steeplechases' are very amusing. A narrow 'racecourse' is arranged along the room, and laid out with obstacles of different heights and at varying distances from each other. The 'obstacles' are made with books, footstools, cushions, and similar objects; but all must be low enough, so as to be easily stepped over.

One of the persons present is blindfolded, and he is challenged to journey from end to end of the course, stepping over all, without touching any of the obstacles. After studying the course he naturally accepts, and he starts on the 'steeplechase'.

As soon as he starts, all the obstacles are quietly and stealthily removed from his path. He advances a few steps, then raises his foot and makes a giant stride over an imaginary obstacle, and as he goes along so ludicrous are his careful efforts to step over non-existent obstacles that everyone is screaming with laughter. The feelings of the misguided steeplechaser when he arrives at the winning-post and discovers the trick that has been played upon him can be better imagined than described.

A 'match-box competition' is one of the funniest games imaginable. Everyone who takes part in it holds an ordinary wooden match-box in the left hand; and whoever first succeeds in extracting a match, striking a light, returning the match when extinguished, and closing the box – all this to be accomplished with the left hand only – becomes the winner, while anyone who uses the right hand is at once disqualified. Strange to say, the instinctive desire to use the right hand in nine competitors out of ten causes them to forget the rule, and so lose the game.

No Christmas party is complete without that laughable sport known as 'cock-fighting' being indulged in. It is played by two people, who seat themselves on the floor, draw their knees towards their chins, suffer their ankles to be bound, and then, clasping their hands over their knees, allow a stick to be inserted beneath the knees and over the arms. Fastened up in this position, the competitors face each other, and on the word being given they endeavour to roll each other over with the tips of their boots.

A 'tug-of-war' is an amusing variation of this game, and endless merriment is caused by the competitors rolling over each other in their efforts for victory.

Henderson's Magazine, 1909–10

CHRISTMAS WITH THE TAILOR

Frank O'Connor

The pleasantest Christmas of my life was spent in the inn in Gougane Barra, though most of the day I was with the Tailor and Anstey. On Christmas Eve the valley was like something out of a fairy-tale, with the still mountain lake mirroring the little white cottages and the little grey fields by day, and at night a hundred candles from a score of cottages. There was only one other visitor at the inn, a middle-aged woman who said she had come there for a quiet holiday. Anstey made great play of that; herself and myself to be all alone in the hotel and no wan at all to oblige the poor woman; what would she think the men of the county were like? The cottage was nearly full after supper, a row of old men sitting on the settle with their hats down over their eyes and their sticks between their knees, while the Tailor sat by the fire in front of them on his butter-box. I brought the whisky and the Tailor supplied the beer. I have never seen the Tailor in better form. He knew I wanted the words and music of a beautiful song which had never been recorded, and he had brought down the only old man in the locality who knew it. The talk began with stories of ghosts and pookas, and then the Tailor sang his favourite song, a version of the Somerset song, 'The Herring'.

> And phwat do you think I made of his belly?
> A lovely girril, her name it was Nelly,
> Sing falderol, falal, falal.
> And what do you think I made of his back?
> A lovely boy, his name it was Jack. . .

Then it was the turn of the other old man, and he hummed and hawed about it.
''Tis a bit barbarous.'
'Even so, even so,' said the Tailor, who had his own way with censorships, ''twasn't you made or composed it.'

> When the evening was fair and the sunlight was yellow

'That's a powerful line,' interjected the singer after the Gaelic words *buidheachtan na gréine*, 'There's a cartload of meaning in that line.'

> When the evening was fair and the sunlight was yellow
> I halted beholding a maiden bright,
> Coming to me by the edge of the mountain;
> Her cheeks had a berry-bright, rosy light;
> The honey-gold hair down her shoulders was twining,
> Swinging and billowing, surging and shining,

Sweeping the grass as she passed by me smiling,
Driving her geese at the fall of night.

The tune was exquisite and there was nothing in the song you could call barbarous except the young woman's warmly expressed objection to sleeping alone instead of having a companion to 'drive the geese' with her. But with the whisky it loosened the tongues of the old men, and they quoted with gusto the supposed dying words of Owen Roe O'Sullivan and told scandalous stories about the neighbours, and then the Tailor sang his party piece about the blacksmith:

John Riordan was well-known in Muskerry
For soldering old iron and the fastening of shoes,
And all the old ladies in the range of the valley
Knew the click of his hammer on their ticky-tack-toos.

Late that night as we stumbled out along the little causeway from the cabin to the road one of the old men slapped me vigorously on the shoulder and roared: 'Well, thanks be to the Almighty God, Frinshias, we had wan grand dirty night.' I admit that at the time I was a little surprised, but, remembering it afterwards, I felt that to thank God for a good uproariously bawdy party was the very hallmark of a deeply religious mind. I don't know, but I commend the idea to moralists.

Leinster, Munster and Connaught, 1950

IRISH SELF-COMMAND

Elizabeth Smith

Xmas day [1840]. . . a dull day, not cold enough. What a pity – I forgot teetotalism when I mixed the puddings, and not one of the outside men would taste them. Now when these unruly people have such self-command where they think it is a sin to yield to temptation, is it not plain that properly educated they would be a fine and a moral race, almost equally plain that those thousand crimes they do commit they have not been taught to consider sins.

The Irish Journal of Elizabeth Smith, 1980

SEASONAL GREETING

James Simmons

Christmas is coming and the afternoons are dark.
The air is Coca-cola-coloured in the public park.
Against the sky the black and shaggy regiments of trees
Are marching. I have bitter thoughts. My bitter thoughts are these:

Christmas is coming and the myths are still alive;
You'd think they would have faded out by nineteen fifty-five.
I never go to church these days, the stories are too queer,
Nor celebrate on Christmas Day the start of Christ's career.

Since you and I by word and deed have shown ourselves heretic,
We need a new philosophy. Oh, isn't it pathetic
To finish with a useless job and not take up another,
But leave the house as usual in case you frighten mother?

Christmas is colouring the chilblain sky with ink,
And every breath of air I draw is cold as an iced drink.
If I were not so brainy, friends, I wouldn't give a damn,
But the common man's so common that I'm bloody glad I am.

In the Wilderness and other Poems, 1969

MIDNIGHT MASS

William Carleton

The Midnight Mass is, no doubt, a phrase familiar to our Irish readers; but we doubt whether those in the sister kingdoms who may honour our book with a perusal would, without a more particular description, clearly understand it.

This ceremony was performed as a commemoration not only of the night, but of the hour in which Christ was born. To connect it either with edification or the abuse of religion would be invidious; so we overlook that, and describe it as it existed within our own memory, remarking, by the way, that though now generally discontinued, it is in some parts of Ireland still observed, or has been till within a few years ago.

The parish in which the scene of this story is laid was large, consequently the attendance of the people was proportionately great. On Christmas day a Roman Catholic priest has, or is said to have, the privilege of saying three masses, though on every other day in the year he can celebrate but two. Each priest, then, said one at midnight, and two on the following day.

Accordingly, about twenty or thirty years ago, the performance of the Midnight Mass was looked upon as an ordinance highly important and interesting. The preparations for it were general and fervent; so much so, that not a Roman Catholic family slept till they heard it. It is true it only occurred once a year; but had any person who saw it once been called upon to describe it, he would say that religion could scarcely present a scene so wild and striking.

The night in question was very dark, for the moon had long disappeared, and as the inhabitants of the whole parish were to meet in one spot, it may be supposed that the difficulty was very great of traversing, in the darkness of midnight, the space between their respective residences and the place appointed by the priest for the celebration of mass. This difficulty they contrived to surmount. From about eleven at night till twelve or one o'clock the parish presented a scene singularly picturesque, and, to a person unacquainted with its causes, altogether mysterious. Over the surface of the surrounding country were scattered myriads of blazing torches, all converging to one point; whilst at a distance, in the central part of the parish, which lay in a valley, might be seen a broad focus of red light, quite stationary, with which one or more of the torches that moved across the fields mingled every moment. These torches were of bog-fir, dried and split for the occasion; all persons were accordingly furnished with them, and by their blaze contrived to make way across the country with comparative ease. This mass having been especially associated with festivity and

137

enjoyment, was always attended by such excessive numbers that the
ceremony was in most parishes celebrated in the open air, if the weather
were at all favourable. Altogether, as we have said, the appearance of
the country at this dead hour of the night was wild and impressive.
Being Christmas, every heart was up, and every pocket replenished
with money, if it could at all be procured. This general elevation of spirits
was nowhere more remarkable than in contemplating the thousands of
both sexes, old and young, each furnished, as before said, with a blazing
flambeau of bog-fir, all streaming down the mountain sides, along the
roads, or across the fields, and settling at last into one broad sheet of fire.
Many a loud laugh might then be heard ringing the night echo into
reverberation; mirthful was the gabble in hard, guttural Irish; and now
and then a song from some one whose potations had been rather
copious would rise on the night breeze, to which a chorus was subjoined
by a dozen voices from the neighbouring groups.

On passing the shebeen and public houses, the din of mingled voices
that issued from them was highly amusing, made up, as it was, of songs,
loud talk, rioting and laughter, with an occasional sound of weeping
from some one who had become penitent in his drink. In the larger
public-houses (for in Ireland there usually are one or two of these in the
immediate vicinity of each chapel) family parties were assembled, who
set in to carouse both before and after mass. Those, however, who had
any love affairs on hand generally selected the shebeen house, as being
private, and less calculated to expose them to general observation. As a
matter of course, these jovial orgies frequently produced such disastrous consequences both to human life and female reputation, that the
intrigues between the sexes, the quarrels, and violent deaths resulting
from them ultimately occasioned the discontinuance of a ceremony
which was only productive of evil. To this day it is an opinion among the

138

peasantry in many parts of Ireland that there is something unfortunate connected with all drinking bouts held upon Christmas Eve. Such a prejudice naturally arises from a recollection of the calamities which so frequently befell many individuals while Midnight Masses were in the habit of being celebrated.

They had now reached the chapel-green, where the scene that presented itself was so striking and strange that we will give the reader an imperfect sketch of its appearance. He who stood at midnight upon a little mount which rose behind the chapel might see between five and six thousand torches, all blazing together, and forming a level mass of red, dusky light, burning against the dark horizon. These torches were so close to each other that their light seemed to blend, as if they had constituted one wide surface of flame; and nothing could be more preternatural looking than the striking and devotional countenances of those who were assembled at their midnight worship, when observed beneath this canopy of fire. The mass was performed under the open sky, upon a table covered with the sacrificial linen and other apparatus for the ceremony. The priest stood, robed in white, with two large torches on each side of his book, reciting the prayers in a low, rapid voice, his hands raised, whilst the congregation were hushed and bent forward in the reverential silence of devotion, their faces touched by the strong blaze of the torches into an expression of deep solemnity. The scenery about the place was wild and striking; and the stars, scattered thinly over the heavens, twinkled with a faint religious light, that blended well with the solemnity of this extraordinary worship, and rendered the rugged nature of the abrupt cliffs and precipices, together with the still outline of the stern mountains, sufficiently visible to add to the wildness and singularity of the ceremony. In fact, there was an unearthly character about it; and the spectre-like appearance of the white-robed priest, as he 'Muttered his prayer to the midnight air,' would almost impress a man with the belief that it was a meeting of the dead, and that the priest was repeating, like the Grey Friar, his 'Mass of the days that were gone.'

On the ceremony being concluded, the scene, however, was instantly changed: the lights were waved and scattered promiscuously among each other, giving an idea of confusion and hurry that was strongly contrasted with the death-like stillness that prevailed a few minutes before. The gabble and laugh were again heard loud and hearty, and the public and shebeen houses once more became crowded. Many of the young people made, on these occasions, what is called 'a runaway'; and other peccadilloes took place, for which the delinquents were either 'read out from the altar', or sent probably to St Patrick's Purgatory at Lough Derg to do penance. Those who did not choose to stop in the whisky houses now hurried home with all speed, to take some sleep before early mass, which was to be performed the next morning about daybreak. The same number of lights might therefore be seen streaming in different ways over the parish; the married men holding the torches, and leading their wives; bachelors escorting their sweethearts, and not unfrequently extinguishing their flambeaux, that the dependence of the females upon their care and protection might more lovingly call forth their gallantry.

The Midnight Mass, 1833

EVENING STAR,
THOU BRINGEST HOME ALL THAT BRIGHT DAWN HATH SCATTERED AFAR, THOU BRINGEST THE SHEEP, THOU BRINGEST THE GOAT, THOU BRINGEST THE CHILD HOME TO THE MOTHER.

CUALA PRESS.

from CAL

Bernard MacLaverty

The next day was Thursday and despite the snow and the state of the roads he went into town early with Dunlop to do his Christmas shopping. He wondered what he could buy for Marcella – something which wouldn't attract questions. Not that he could afford much. He bought her a tiny bottle of perfume which cost him the best part of three days' wages and in a bookshop he asked if they had any books by or about the artist who had so impressed her. The assistant gave him a small paperback of Grünewald's paintings and he slipped it into his pocket. He bought Shamie a bottle of after-shave and a shaving stick, as he had done every year since he could remember. They seemed to last exactly from Christmas to Christmas. He also bought his father a one-thousand piece jigsaw to cheer him up. When Cal was a child Shamie had always interfered over his shoulder, wanting to put pieces into his jigsaws. In the toy shop he saw some 'Raggedy Anne' dolls flopped against the wall with their heads pitched forward like drunks. He bought one for Lucy.

Outside, the Preacher stood at the corner shouting at the top of his voice about God. He wore a black plastic apron with the words 'Repent ye; for the kingdom of heaven is at hand'. There was no one listening to him except a few of his cronies, also wearing black bibs, who were standing up against the wall. Everyone else bustled past, some even stepping into the slush of the gutter to avoid him. He windmilled his arms and shouted as Cal passed him. 'Without the shedding of blood there can be no forgiveness.'

'Good evening,' said Cal.

He got no answer from Dermot Ryan's front door so he went round the back and found it open. He went in, kicking the snow off his shoes, and called for Shamie but there was no answer. He sat down to wait. Perhaps they had both gone out for a drink. If they had, it was a good sign. He took out the paperback of the paintings and began to look through it. He heard the front door open and shouted a warning that he was in. Dermot opened the door by himself.

'Where's Shamie?'

'He was worse than they thought, Cal. The doctor put him in for treatment.'

'Where?'

'Gransha.'

'Oh God, no.'

'They say this electrical shock treatment is bad. Very hard on you.'

'How the hell am I supposed to get to Derry to see him?'

Dermot shrugged and sat down, readjusting his cap on his head.

Briefly Cal saw the track of the headband on the little hair that Dermot had.

'What about the van? Where is it?'

'A boy at the abattoir has it.'

'Crilly?'

'Aye, I think so.'

'Jesus.'

'Too generous for his own good. He's some man, your father. It broke my heart to see the way he was. Like iron to plasticine overnight.' He sat close to the fire, the top buttons of his trousers undone making a white V on his pot belly. One hand was on his knee, the other hooked in his braces.

'Cal, the world is full of gulpins who don't care who they hurt.'

'Will he be out for Christmas?'

'I doubt it – from what the doctor said.'

Cal went over to the table where he had left the presents.

'If you see him, will you give him this?' he said and handed the large box to Dermot. 'And there's a present for yourself for putting up with him.' He gave Dermot the wrapped after-shave and stick. 'It's the same brand as Shamie uses and I got to like the smell of it.'

'Thanks, Cal. You're as like your father as two peas in a pod.'

He went to the library to pass the time and was disappointed and annoyed when he saw the bespectacled figure of the head librarian behind the desk instead of Marcella. If he had thought about it for a moment he would have realised that with nobody to mind her child in the evening she would not be on duty. Now he would have to walk home, or hitch-hike, which was dangerous.

He wandered down to the section which had the cartoon books and opened one – a selection from the *New Yorker*. A voice behind him said,

'Good to see you, Cal.'

He froze and without looking he knew it was Crilly.

'I didn't expect to see you in a place like this,' said Cal, turning to face him. The big man stood smiling, his head hanging to make him look less tall.

'Why not?'

'I read one book in school. That was one more than you.'

'The books is not for me. Here, c'mere.'

He led Cal over to the fiction section and cocked his head to the side. He ran his finger along the titles and tapped a fat book. *Middlemarch* by George Eliot. Cal said, –

'So what?'

'There's plenty in that book,' said Crilly. He took it out very gently and looked all around him and, seeing no one, flipped open the cover. There was a square hole cut in the pages. Inside was a small bag of

142

powder wired to a watch. Crilly closed the book carefully and slipped it back onto the shelf. He said,

'I don't borrow books. I bring them in.'

'Jesus, why do you want to burn down a library?'

'Government property, isn't it? Orders is orders, Cal.'

'Fuckin' hell.'

Call turned away from him but Crilly gripped his arm.

'Skeffington would like a word with you.' He added, 'Urgent.'

'I'm not interested any more.'

'We've been looking all over for you. I heard you were in England.'

'No, I'm still around.'

Crilly's hand remained on his arm.

'Where?'

'Here.'

The librarian looked over his glasses to see who was speaking so loudly. Crilly smiled and reduced his voice to a whisper close to Cal's ear.

'Now, Cal, don't fuck me about. Where are you living at?'

'Outside town.'

'Let's go to my house and Skeffington can drop in and see us, eh?' Cal shrugged. Crilly's voice had turned friendly but Cal knew that he shouldn't go. He allowed himself to be led out of the library and on to the street. Crilly walked very close to him. He asked him what was in the present and Cal told him it was a doll. Cal thought of running but it seemed so stupid to run away from this guy he had been to school with.

Cal, 1983

CHRISTMAS IN OLD DUBLIN 3

Annie M.P. Smithson

From very early times Thomas Street was a great place for street markets. W.A. Henderson, writing in a Dublin paper about twenty-three years ago, describes the market in these words:

My first experience of the Market was in 1878. About three days before Christmas the country carts began to arrive, laden with slaughtered fowl, and took up their positions on the south side of the street – a long line extending from James's Street up to and often into High Street, numbering from fifty to a hundred. The horses were unyoked and taken to stables and yards. The shafts were lowered, and usually an old country woman took her seat on this elevation, with all the skewered fowl laid out on the straw. There she dictated the terms of purchase. There was continuous haggling and a good deal of humour and teazing – besides blessing and cursing. For the time being the cart is her home; here she sleeps under a large, faded umbrella, and here she has brought to her breakfast, dinner and tea. She makes herself comfortable with a couple of heavy shawls and a multiplication of petticoats, and from her seat she will not move except on the stress of necessity. In some cases the old farmer would mount guard while his wife and daughter ran across the street to Jacob's Restaurant for their meals.

'When the weather was fine and business good the life was pleasant enough, and the old country folk enjoyed the experience, in spite of the prolonged sitting on the slanting platforms. But sometimes it would be frosty and bitterly cold and the sellers would be nearly frozen in their seats. A heavy snowstorm would bury sellers and birds under its white mantle, but worst of all was the winter's rain, with a pitiless cold soaking into the very skin.

'Though sales might be slack in the daytime, the night time made amends. There was a mighty throng in Thomas Street during the great days of the Fair, with any amount of sport, jostling and shouting, horseplay, and unfortunately a good deal of drinking. The shops were all brilliantly lit up, and kept open till a late hour. There were many booths in the street illuminated with kerosene lamps, and also blazing 'duck-lamps'. There would be great displays of cheap Christmas toys and cards and presents, cooking utensils and certain kinds of food. Huge heaps of holly and ivy were piled in the streets and mistletoe was not wanting. Large 'corncrakes' were swung around, making a hideous din, and boys blew lustily on bugles and horns.

'The Christmas Eve Market was especially interesting. A large number of buyers postponed their purchase till the last moment in the hope of getting a big bargain. The seller did not want to lose the chance

of a sale, but she also wanted to get as much as possible. The play between the two was worth watching, and some of the dialogue was delicious. A dozen times the buyer would depart, only to be called back again until a settlement was reached.'

The writer finished this interesting account by saying:

'The great Christmas Market in Thomas Street, which had been dwindling for years, is now a thing of the past. Last year, on Christmas Eve, I walked down the almost deserted street. Not a single turkey or goose was to be seen where once a thousand were annually laid out in state. There were about six small tables fitted out with a few skewered rabbits and as many miserable fowl. That was all. What was the cause of this downfall? The new generation of farmers perhaps did not approve of street sales; more probably the business was better organised, and poulterers made direct contracts for all the fowl that the farmers could produce, or the business may have been taken up by whosesale dealers. But from whatever cause, the Christmas Market in Thomas Street came to an end and will soon be forgotten.'

'Christmas in Old Dublin'. *Dublin Historical Record*, 1943

SAINT BRIDE'S LULLABY AT BETHLEHEM

Cathal O'Byrne

Sleep sweetly, sleep featly, O, Little Gold Head!
With the ox and the ass in their cold, dank shed,
Bride watches over Your breath-warmed bed,
Flower o' the World,
Shoheen, sho-ho.

Sing lightly if brightly, O, Little Brown Bird!
Above on the rafter, nor loudly be heard,
So the sleep of Our Birdeen be peaceful, unstirred,
In His yellow nest curled,
A leanaván Ó!

Mother Mary is weary, the starry night through
She cuddled You close in Her mantle of blue,
Now Your wee Foster-mother keeps watch over You
Without fear or fail,
Husheen, husho.

Erin keeps guard for Mary, 'tis Her Son's divine plan,
Sharing sorrow for sorrow, since sorrow began,
And leal is her love while a woman or man
Shall remain of the Gael,
A Íosagán, O!

Christmas Wayfarers, 1932

THE CAROL-SINGERS

J.D. Sheridan

We had our first carol-singers the other night, although it is a good three weeks before Christmas, and from now on there will be no rest for a man with small change in his pocket – unless he is strong-minded enough to ignore knocks, or patient enough to sit in darkness and so avoid them altogether. I am not against carol-singers, but I think that nowadays they come too early and too often. When I was young, carol-singers were sudden and seldom – like snow, or a piper's band. They waited until the very brink of the feast, and were not far in front of the herald angels. They worked on a short tether, too, and never ventured outside their own parish, but nowadays carol-singers map out fresh districts like burglars, so that you may have to pay hush-money to several contingents on the same night.

On this subject, as on so many others, the Littlest One doesn't agree with me. She thinks that the carol-singers couldn't come too early or too often, that they should begin immediately after Hallow Eve and keep whacking away till Little Christmas. For the past fortnight she has been putting a tiny addendum to her night prayers, and it comes as she rises off her knees – showing that her mind cannot be wholly on her orisons. She says 'I hope the carol-singers will come to-night,' and sometimes she adds: 'Hadn't we a fire in the chimney once when I was small?' If she could have the fire brigade and the carol-singers on the same night her cup would be full.

She likes the carol-singers because they have a licence to do all the things that a respectable young lady, once abed, would like to do but daren't – to knock at all the doors, and waken all the babies, and frighten all the birds. She wants the night to be filled with music, and so, at this time of year, she lies awake listening and is as intent as a rabbit at the mouth of his burrow. She may be deceived, though never for long, by barking dogs or singing errand boys, but she knows her own when they come, and after that there is no danger of falling asleep.

The real beauty of carol-singing from her point of view is that it overlaps in each direction. It works up to a slow crescendo, holds its climax for fully five minutes, and then fades slowly in the distance until the far-away door-knockings could be overlain by the scratching of a mouse behind the wardrobe. It is not a fierce and short-lived joy, like a passing fire-engine: it lasts as long as a slab of sticky toffee. It gives the tumultuous, agitated heart time to settle down again, and when the last knock comes fairy-faint from the farthest house in all the world, the Littlest One is soothed and ready for sleep.

Funnily Enough, 1956

A PRESENT FOR CHRISTMAS

Bernard MacLaverty

McGettigan woke in the light of midday, numb with the cold. He had forgotten to close the door the night before and his coat had slipped off him onto the boards of the floor. He swivelled round on the sofa and put the overcoat on, trying to stop shivering. At his feet there was a dark green wine bottle and his hand shook as he reached out to test its weight. He wondered if he had had the foresight to leave a drop to warm himself in the morning. It was empty and he flung it in the corner with the others, wincing at the noise of the crash.

He got to his feet and buttoned the only button on his coat. The middle section he held together with his hands thrust deep in his pockets and went out into the street putting his head down against the wind. He badly needed something to warm him.

His hand searched for his trouser pocket without the hole. There was a crumpled pound and what felt like a fair amount of silver. He was all right. Nobody had fleeced him the night before. Yesterday he had got his Christmas money from the Assistance and he had what would cure him today, with maybe something left for Christmas Day itself.

Strannix's bar was at the back of the Law Courts about two minutes from McGittigan's room but to McGettigan it seemed like an eternity. His thin coat flapped about his knees. He was so tall he always thought he got the worst of the wind. When he pushed open the door of the bar he felt the wave of heat and smoke and spirit smells surround him like a hug. He looked quickly behind the bar. Strannix wasn't on. It was only the barman, Hughie – a good sort. McGettigan went up to the counter and stood shivering. Hughie set him up a hot wine without a word. McGettigan put the money down on the marble slab but Hughie gestured it away.

'Happy Christmas, big lad,' he said. McGettigan nodded still unable to speak. He took the steaming glass, carrying it in both hands, to a bench at the back of the bar, and waited a moment until it cooled a bit. Then he downed it in one. He felt his insides unfurl and some of the pain begin to disappear. He got another one which he paid for.

After the second the pains had almost gone and he could unbend his long legs, look up and take in his surroundings. It was past two by the bar clock and there was a fair number in the bar. Now he saw the holly and the multi-coloured decorations and the HAPPY XMAS written white on the mirror behind the bar. There was a mixture of people at the counter, locals and ones in from the Law Courts with their waistcoats and sharp suits. They were wise-cracking and laughing and talking between each other which didn't happen every day of the year. With Strannix off he could risk going up to the bar. You never know what could happen. It was the sort of day a man could easily get drink bought for him.

He stood for a long time smiling at their jokes but nobody took any notice of him so he bought himself another hot wine and went back to his seat. It was funny how he'd forgotten that it was so near Christmas. One day was very much the same as another. Long ago Christmases had been good. There had been plenty to eat and drink. A chicken, vegetables and spuds, all at the same meal, ending up with plum-duff and custard. Afterwards the Da, if he wasn't too drunk, would serve out the mulled claret. He would heat a poker until it glowed red and sparked white when bits of dust hit it as he drew it from the fire – that was another thing, they'd always had a fire at Christmas – then he'd plunge it down the neck of the bottle and serve the wine out in cups with a spoonful of sugar in the bottom of each. Then they knew that they could go out and play with their new things until midnight if they liked, because the Ma and the Da would get full and fall asleep in the chairs. By bedtime their new things were always broken but it didn't seem to matter because you could always do something with them. Those were the days.

But there were bad times as well. He remembered the Christmas day he ended lying on the cold lino, crying in the corner, sore from head to foot after a beating the Da had given him. He had knocked one of the figures from the crib on the mantelpiece and it smashed to white plaster bits on the hearth. The Da had bought the crib the day before and was a bit the worse for drink and he had laid into him with the belt – buckle and all. Even now he couldn't remember which figure it was.

McGettigan was glad he wasn't married. He could get full whenever he liked without children to worry about. He was his own master. He could have a good Christmas. He searched his pockets and took out all his money and counted it. He could afford a fair bit for Christmas Day. He knew he should get it now, just in case, and have it put to one side. Maybe he could get something to eat as well.

He went up to the counter and Hughie leaned over to hear him above the noise of the bar. When McGettigan asked him for a carry-out Hughie reminded him that it was only half-past two. Then McGettigan explained that he wanted it for Christmas. Three pint bottles of stout and three of wine.

'Will this do?' asked Hughie holding up the cheapest wine in the place and smiling. He put the bottles in a bag and left it behind the counter.

'You'll tell the boss it's for me, if he comes in,' said McGettigan.

'If Strannix comes in you'll be out on your ear,' Hughie said.

Strannix was a mean get and everybody knew it. He hated McGettigan, saying that he was the type of customer he could well do without. People like him got the place a bad name. What he really meant was that

149

the judges and lawyers, who drank only the dearest and best – and lots of it – might object to McGettigan's sort. Strannix would strangle his grandmother for a halfpenny. It was a standing joke in the bar for the lawyers, when served with whiskey, to say, 'I'll just put a little more water in this.' Strannix was an out-and-out crook. He not only owned the bar but also the houses of half the surrounding streets. McGettigan paid him an exorbitant amount for his room and although he hated doing it he paid as regularly as possible because he wanted to hold onto this last shred. You were beat when you didn't have a place to go. His room was the last thing he wanted to lose.

Now that he was feeling relaxed McGettigan got himself a stout and as he went back to his seat he saw Judge Boucher come in. Everybody at the bar wished him a happy Christmas in a ragged chorus. One young lawyer having wished him all the best, turned and rolled his eyes and sniggered into his hot whiskey.

Judge Boucher was a fat man, red faced with a network of tiny broken purple veins. He wore a thick, warm camel-hair overcoat and was peeling off a pair of fur-lined gloves. McGettigan hadn't realized he was bald the first time he had seen him because then he was wearing his judge's wig and sentencing him to three months for drunk and disorderly. McGettigan saw him now tilt his first gin and tonic so far back that the lemon slice hit his moustache. He slid the glass back to Hughie who refilled it. Judge Boucher cracked and rubbed his hands together and said something about how cold it was, then he pulled a piece of paper from his pocket and handed it to Hughie with a wad of money. The judge seemed to be buying for those around him so McGettigan went up close to him.

'How're ye Judge,' he said. McGettigan was a good six inches taller than the judge, but round shouldered. The judge turned and looked up at him.

'McGettigan. Keeping out of trouble, eh?' he said.

'Yis, sur. But things is bad at the minute. . . like. . . you know how it is. Now if I had the money for a bed. . .' said McGettigan fingering the stubble of his chin.

'I'll buy you no drink,' snapped the judge. 'That's the cause of your trouble, man. You look dreadful. How long is it since you've eaten?'

'It's not the food your lordship. . .' began McGettigan but he was interrupted by the judge ordering him a meat pie. He took it with mumbled thanks and went back to his seat once again.

'Happy Christmas,' shouted the judge across the bar.

Just then Strannix came in behind the bar. He was a huge muscular man and had his sleeves rolled up to his biceps. He talked in a loud Southern brogue. When he spied McGettigan he leaned over the bar hissing, 'Ya skinney big hairpin. I thought I told you if ever I caught

150

you. . .'

'Mr Strannix,' called the judge from the other end of the counter. Strannix's face changed from venom to smile as he walked the duck-boards to where the judge stood.

'Yes Judge what can I do for you?' he said. The judge had now become the professional.

'Let him be,' he said. 'Good will to all men and all that.' He laughed loudly and winked in McGettigan's direction. Strannix filled the judge's glass again and stood with a fixed smile waiting for the money.

At four o'clock the judge's car arrived for him and after much hand-shaking and backslapping he left. McGettigan knew his time had come. Strannix scowled over at him and with a vicious gesture of his big thumb, ordered him out.

'Hughie has a parcel for me,' said McGettigan defiantly, '. . . and it's paid for,' he added before Strannix could ask. Strannix grabbed the paper bag, then came round the counter and shoved it into McGettigan's arms and guided him firmly out the door. As the door closed McGettigan shouted, 'I hope this Christmas is your last.'

The door opened again and Strannix stuck his big face out. 'If you don't watch yourself I'll be round for the rent,' he snarled.

McGettigan spat on the pavement loud enough for Strannix to hear. It was beginning to rain and the dark sky seemed to bring on the night more quickly. McGettigan clutched his carry-out in the crook of his arm, his exposed hand getting cold. Then he sensed something odd about the shape in the bag. There was a triangular shape in there. Not a shape he knew.

He stopped at the next street light and opened the bag. There was a bottle of whiskey, triangular in section. There was also a bottle of vodka, two bottles of gin, a bottle of brandy and what looked like some tonic.

He began to run as fast as he could. He was in bad shape, his breath rasped in his throat, his boots were filled with lead, his heart moved up and thumped in his head. As he ran he said a frantic prayer that they wouldn't catch him.

Once inside his room he set his parcel gently on the sofa, snibbed the door and lay against it panting and heaving. When he got his breath back he hunted the yard, in the last remaining daylight, for some nails he knew were in a tin. Then he hammered them through the door into the jamb with wild swings of a hatchet. Then he pushed the sofa against the door and looked around the room. There was nothing else that could be moved. He sat down on the floor against the wall at the window and lined the bottles in front of him. Taking them out they tinked like full bells. In silence he waited for Strannix.

Within minutes he came, he and Judge Boucher stamping into the hallway. They battered on the door, shouting his name. Strannix shouted, 'McGettigan. We know you're in there. If you don't come out I'll kill you.'

The judge's voice tried to reason. 'I bought you a meat pie, McGettigan.' He sounded genuinely hurt.

But his voice was drowned by Strannix.

'McGettigan, I know you can hear me. If you don't hand back that parcel I'll get you evicted.' There was silence. Low voices conferred outside the door. Then Strannix shouted again. 'Evicted means put out, you stupid hairpin.'

Then after some more shouting and pummelling on the door they went away, their mumbles and footsteps fading gradually.

McGettigan laughed as he hadn't laughed for years, his head thrown back against the wall. He played eeny-meeny-miney-mo with the bottles in front of him – and the whiskey won. The click of the metal seal breaking he thought much nicer than the pop of a cork. He teased himself by not drinking immediately but got up and, to celebrate, put a shilling in the meter to light the gas fire. Its white clay sections were broken and had all fallen to the bottom. The fire banged loudly because it had not been lit for such a long time, making him jump and laugh. Then McGettigan pulled the sofa up to the fire and kicked off his boots. His toes showed white through the holes in his socks and the steam began to rise from his feet. A rectangle of light fell on the floor from the streetlamp outside the uncurtained window. The whiskey was red and gold in the light from the gas fire.

He put the bottle to his head and drank. The heat from inside him met the warmth of his feet and they joined in comfort. Again and again he put the bottle to his head and each time he lowered it he listened to the music of the back-slop. Soon the window became a bright diamond and he wondered if it was silver rain drifting in the halo of the lamp or if it was snow for Christmas. Choirs of boy sopranos sang carols and McGettigan, humming, conducted slowly with his free hand and the room bloomed in the darkness of December.

Secrets and other Stories, 1977

WREN BOYS
Jack B. Yeats

A CHRISTMAS CARD

John Montague

Christmas in Brooklyn,
the old El flashes by.
A man plods along pulling
his three sons on a sleigh;
soon his whole family
will vanish away.

My long lost father
trudging home through
this strange, cold city,
its whirling snows,
unemployed and angry
living off charity.

Finding a home only
in brother John's speakeasy.
Beneath the stoup
a flare of revelry.
And yet you found time
to croon to your last son.

Dear father, a gracenote.
That Christmas, you did
find a job, guarding a
hole in the navy yard.
Elated, you celebrated
so well, you fell in.

Not a model father.
I was only happy
when I was drunk
you said, years later,
building a fire in
a room I was working in.

Still, you soldiered on
all those years alone in
a Brooklyn boarding house
without your family
until the job was done;
and then limped home.

The Dead Kingdom, 1984

Seajan · mac Catmaoil · del.

CHRISTMASTIDE

Peig Sayers

By this time Christmas was not far away and this is the time of great hustle and bustle for townspeople. On the Saturday before Christmas the street was black with people: they were like harvest midges moving in and out through each other, collecting 'commands' as they went from house to house and a good number of the men with their hats on the sides of their heads as a result of their having a jorum taken. I thought that there weren't so many people in the world as were gathered into the house at that hour of day! Such argument and uproar and discussion! The taproom was a solid mass of people; in the middle of the floor stood a great long table with forms on either side of it and the people were so crushed together that a tiny wren wouldn't have found room to move among them. One man was singing and another was talking: I wasn't listening to anyone but to Micil Thomáisín singing *Bó na bPúcai* – 'The Fairy Cow' – a song made by Poet Dunlea. This was a song mocking the peelers:

> A Captain Cinders who ne'er saw battle
> From Ballygoleen despatched with cattle
> A pair of peelers with strict citation
> To make 'Ferriter Dunes their destination.
> On their journey there they passed resolution
> At Tavern Hoare to make dissolution
> And while they'd loiter and have their spree
> On the road the cattle could wander free.

Every time he finished a verse the rest of the company would raise this yell that'd knock echoes out of the loft over their heads. After a while a man stuck down his head.

'I own to God, Micil,' he said, 'wouldn't a scrap o' sense be better to you than that nourishment! The Brass Buttons are outside!'

155

THE GREAT SKELLIG.

'Let them go to hell, son,' Micil said, and he raised his voice in another verse:

As they entered the bar and the maid instructed
The Gentle People a cow abducted;
With magical hues they began to size her
Till no peeler born could recognize her.
They bore her aloft in a whirl of mist
By breezes from Marhan and Clasach kissed.
She now yields milk in creamy spillage
In a fort to the north of O'Dorney Village.

Before long Beit his wife, came in. 'Miraculous God!' she said, 'have any of ye seen this Micil of mine?'

'I'm here, girl; come on down,' said Micil.

She got a welcome and she took her seat at the end of the bench.

'You'll drink a drop now,' said Micil, 'and then we'll head for home.'

'Wisha,' says Beit, 'isn't it bad enough for one of us to be cracked without having the pair of us in the one trim.'

Micil stood up and filled a glass out of a jug that stood on the table. Beit was trying to refuse the drink.

'Here, girl!' he said raising another blast of a song:

156

Your health, my friend, and drain your glass
Our common welfare will come to pass!

and he began his song all over again.

The peelers were busy outside because at that time there was great agitation among the people. The Land Question was still very much to the fore and the unfortunate tenants were being sorely harried by the landlords. Like every other place a branch of the Land League had been established in Dingle and many people were starting to take part in the Plan of Campaign, and as a result of this, here and there a person was being boycotted. So the peelers had their hands full, especially in any locality where there were drinkers and spouters for they had the suspicion that whatever secret or privacy topers held they'd maybe let it slip out in their talk when their wits were astray. But take my word for it, the people were very cautious and they'd give the 'Brassies' the least opportunity possible.

However, Micil was in full cry when, in the final verse of the song, two policemen hopped in the door, and grabbing poor Micil, they hoisted him off to the barracks. That was the first person I had ever seen being arrested by the authorities.

The house was then like a grave; not a hum nor a haw out of anyone and those present began to drift off quietly. No one felt the situation as keenly as Beit because now she had no one to guide the horse home and she was troubled in her mind and very upset.

'Pull yourself together!' Séamas, the man of the house, told her. 'The night will be fine and bright and if all goes to all they can't keep him inside beyond ten o'clock. Muiris Bán and myself will go the barracks and get him released at ten.' The poor woman calmed down then.

About ten o'clock Séamas and Muiris went off and brought Micil back with them. He was your subdued man! When he came in the door to us with a class of a foolish smirk on his face, Beit said, ''Tis easily known that your throat would land you in trouble, my hayro!'

'Shut up now!' said Micil. 'Can't I boast that I was taken to the barracks without any charge being laid against me except that I was singing! Get ready straightaway and believe you me, too, the black mare won't be long covering the road north.'

They said good-bye to us and I daresay they weren't idle until they reached home.

Peig: the Autobiography of Peig Sayers of the Great Blasket Islands, 1974

from THE BREAD GOD

John Montague

He who stood at mightnight upon a little mount which rose behind the chapel, might see between five and six thousand torches, all blazing together, and forming a level mass of red dusky light, burning against the horizon. These torches were so close to each other that their light seemed to blend, as if they had constituted one wide surface of flame; and nothing could be more preternatural looking than the striking and devotional countenance of those who were assembled at their midnight worship, when observed beneath this canopy of fire. . .

Christmas Morning

> Lights outline a hill
> As silently the people,
> Like shepherd and angel
> On that first morning,
> March from Altcloghfin,
> Beltany, Rarogan,
> Under rimed hawthorn,
> Gothic evergreen,
> Grouped in the warmth
> & cloud of their breath,
> Along cattle paths
> Crusted with ice,
> Tarred roads to this
> Gray country chapel
> Where a gas-lamp hisses
> To light the crib
> Under the cross-beam's
> Damp flaked message:
> GLORIA IN EXCELSIS.

Yes, I remember Carleton's description of Christmas in Tyrone, but things had changed at the end of the century. Religion was at a pretty low ebb in those days. We had one Mass at 10 o'clock on Sundays at which a handful went to communion. We went to confession and communion about every four months. The priests did not take much interest in the people and did not visit them except for sick calls. I think I became a priest because we were the most respectable family in the parish and it was expected of me, but what I really wanted to do was to join the army, which was out of the question. So you see how your uncle became a Jesuit!

Christmas, Melbourne, 1960

The Rough Field, 1972

THE SPIRIT OF CHRISTMAS

Donal Foley

Mr S. Claus (192) of no fixed abode, appeared yesterday in the Dublin District Court before District Justice Nell McCafferty charged with breaking and entry and riotous behaviour. A garda said that Claus was found trying to get down a chimney of a house in the Foxrock district of Dublin. He had a large selection of wrapped-up objects which he could not account for. He smelled strongly of drink and insisted on singing 'Away in a Manger'.

The District Justice asked if anything was known about Claus. The garda said he had given trouble before at this time of the year. Chimneys seemed to have a fascination for him. He was a well-known eccentric in the Catholic districts of Dublin. Also, he was constantly in the company of Miss Dicey Reilly, who was also a constant trouble with the Gardai. Reilly, who subsequently appeared before the court, was accused of being drunk and disorderly and refusing to fight. She admitted to the Justice that she had a sup taken, but could not give it up.

Judge McCafferty said it was quite clear that both defendants were victims of society and seemed to be taking pleasure in it. She felt, however, that a suspended sentence of two years in Purgatory would meet the situation. She warned them both that if they appeared before her again, they would be sent straight to Hell. Claus swayed and collapsed in the dock. He was handed over to the Sick and Indignant Roomkeepers Society. The District Justice asked for psychiatric reports as soon as possible.

Man Bites Dog, 1975

A KERRY CHRISTMAS

Brendan Kennelly

The frost transfigures and the wind deceives,
A warring season bickers to its end,
The exiles gather and the land believes
It knows a birth, commemorates a friend
Who scatters crumbs of love to north and south,
Countering the scrounging winter light;
Goodwill dribbles from the swilling mouth,
The mad Atlantic thrashes in the night

Where Mollie Conner, shawled in total black,
The smell of clay telling where she has been,
A cross of generation on her back,
Nourished by the long, resurgent story
Explaining what ecstatic voices mean,
Stumbles to her private, certain glory.

Selected Poems, 1969

160

THE CHRISTMAS TREE

Jennifer Johnston

Bill brought the tree.

I was sitting at my little table by the fire trying to concentrate, to gather my wandering thoughts, to mould together the images pressing into the front of my mind and the words that gave them some sort of meaning.

'Typing, I see.'

He came into the room carrying the tree in front of him. The beautiful smell of pine needles filled the room.

'You see what an obedient animal I am. As ordered, one tree.'

He put it down on the floor and we had a look at it. A good compact tree, neat, no straggling branches. Just the tree I would have chosen myself. He had wedged it into a round brass pot.

'It's lovely. Really lovely. Thank you, Bill.'

'Where will I put it?'

'On that table there in the window. You are good. I hope it wasn't too much bother.'

'What on earth are you wearing those peculiar clothes for?'

I realised I was still dressed in the boots and overcoat.

'Oh. . .'

'I hope you weren't thinking of going out. I would be very, very angry if you did a silly thing like that.'

'I just put them on for fun.'

'A likely tale. Ooops.'

He lifted the tree on to the table.

'Doesn't that look marvellous? Have you got decorations and all that?'

'Somewhere. I'll look later. I feel terribly excited. If I were still at school, I'd write an essay called My Last Christmas Tree.'

He laughed.

'Dreadful woman.'

'Will you have a cup of coffee? I haven't the foggiest idea what the time is.'

'No, thanks. I'm doing my rounds, and everything's a bit hectic. Sit down and let me take those things off your feet.'

I sat down. Gently he pulled off each boot and stood them side by side on the floor.

'You looked as if you were going to drown in them. You must have energy today. Typing, drowning in boots, you've even cleaned the place up a bit. What are you typing, or should I ask?'

I leaned back in the chair and looked at the tree.

'I thought maybe I could sort a few things out for myself. I've always been led to believe that an awareness. . .'

In the Pine Forest it had been so silent that you could hear the needles slithering to the ground, the distant musical whisper of water.

'Awareness?'

He was rubbing bark stain off one of his hands with his handkerchief.

'I thought that the urgency of it all might make my mind clear. Show me a pattern of some sort. "Depend upon it, sir, when a man knows he is to be hanged in a fortnight, it concentrates his mind wonderfully." One great saying proved wrong. I find myself lost in a forest of irrelevancies.'

'You're not going to be hanged in a fortnight.'

'Don't let's be too literal about it.'

'Who said that anyway? It's vaguely familiar.'

'I don't really remember. You'd better go and look after your patients. The flu, the measles and the problems of the lower back. I will decorate the tree. Tomorrow you can come and admire it. . . and give yourself time to stay and have a drink.'

'Yes. I'll do that. Can I get your slippers or something to put on your feet?'

'I'm all right.'

'The floor is cold.'

'I'll get them later. You run along.'

He touched my shoulder with a finger. A few small green needles from the tree clung to the sleeve of his coat.

'Thank you, Bill.'

The Christmas Tree, 1981

THE CHRISTMAS FESTIVAL

Michael J. Murphy

Christmas brought a festival of holiness and tradition. Lighted candles are still placed in every window. This is a symbol of traditional hospitality to unfortunate wayfarers; and while it signifies the Light which Christ brought into the world, it proclaims the people's undying memory of the time when Mary and Joseph were refused shelter in Bethlehem. It expressses, too, the characteristic hope of those with exiles far away that they shall see them again before taking to their death-bed.

Another tradition associated with the spirit of Christmas, though not actually occurring on that date, was that known as 'The Feast of the Twelve Candles', which was observed on the Epiphany, with a candle for each day since the passing of Christmas. In early days, resin-sluts were used, although some people will observe it by using ordinary candles. The lights were lit and arranged in a circle, and the family recited the Rosary while kneeling around the lights.

The old market of Christmas was known as 'the Marra-ga-more' or 'Big Market Day'. 'Humpy Thursday' was Newry Market Day, while 'Humpy Monday' was the nickname given to Dundalk Market Day. Everyone was 'humpy' with parcels on their backs.

People started for the market while the stars were still in the sky. Men, women and girls walked with their donkeys and creels 'to make their markets' – then an integral part of any girl's training. Stalls, or 'stan'ins' were placed outside shops, and great excitement prevailed as shopmen tried to coax or persuade the throngs of buyers to purchase goods. The people had many pairs of knitted socks for especial sale on this day. Old men and women relished 'half-ones' of whiskey. People usually dealt steadily in certain shops, and were presented in December with Christmas boxes of food and cakes, with a calendar bearing the shopman's name and trade, some whiskey, and two large candles for lighting in the windows at home. Some traders gave presents equal to every person's Christmas purchases. Then in a merry mood, the people – the women anyhow – came home on the back of the donkeys with their wares in baskets or in the creels. They took the old roads and sang in communal chorus old songs and ballads.

The Christmas pudding was made principally of potatoes and bread some days before the Feast. It was cooked in a calico bag which was suspended in the pot by a cord tied to the crook. The boiling took an hour and a half alone. On Christmas Eve, it was cut, and toasts of whiskey drank. Men went from one house to another, wishing goodwill and treating people with whiskey, with everyone returning the compliments. Go-betweens settled quarrels and differences between 'those at variance', and the whole night was spent in active and reciprocal visits singing and merry-making.

A man liked to entertain his guests by dancing a jig over crossed belts or across Christmas plates [willow patterned dishes] placed in four-leaved shamrock form on the floor. The dancer held a pot-stick which he passed from hand to hand in various ways. Exceptionally light-footed dancers could do a treble toe-tattoo actually on a plate even in their heavy boots.

At Slieve Gullion's Foot, 1975

CAROL SINGERS
for Deirdre

John Hewitt

Why should it stir me, when, each face intent,
the Christmas children sing my childhood back,
clustered with hollied memories, innocent,
   that lie discarded on my lonely track?

The walk in frost and darkness to the church,
doubling my steps to match my father's stride,
the greetings and the handshakes in the porch –
   he held that faith, I think, until he died.

That faith, that story, half the stuff of art,
   the myth, the magic of the Holy Child –
why should such sadness gather round my heart,
   when every sense reports it unfulfilled,
     its terms decayed, its uses out of date
as easel-painting or my classroom slate?

Out of My Time, 1974

A PRECOCIOUS CHILD

Maeve Binchy

When I was young and spoiled and indulged, instead of being old and spoiled and indulged, I decided late one Christmas Eve that I was going to cancel all previous letters to Santa Claus and ask him for a doll's house.

Laboriously and apologetically I wrote all this to Himself and put it up the chimney and retired happily, leaving confusion and sadness amongst those who had bought me a lovely blackboard and 50 pieces of chalk.

A child's Christmas couldn't be ruined, they told each other, but on the other hand all the shops were closed and doll's houses were out. So they tried to make one. For hours and hours, I believe, they laboured on a big box and painted it white and drew windows in it and stuck on chimneys that kept falling off. One of the few rows of their married life developed over the inability to construct a simple thing like a doll's house.

'Boys should have learned carpentry at school,' said my mother in despair as the front of the house caved in yet again.

'Women should know about toys,' countered my father as he got out the glue pot once more.

Then they thought about straw and making a doll's house, Hawaian style, but this might not be a good idea in case I hadn't heard of Polynesian houses.

'With all the money we pay at that expensive school, they should have taught her that,' said my father. But the straw was damp anyway, so that was abandoned.

A doll's igloo with cotton wool as snow was considered and abandoned. A doll's tepee seemed a good idea if they could paint a doll up as an Indian to go with it. But it required bark, skins, or canvas, and so they had to give that up, too, since they had been thinking of making it with a sheet.

They ruminated wistfully about my younger sister then, and now, easier to please in life, who would be delighted with a rattle or a teddy bear or even nothing at all.

'To be fair,' said my father, 'she *is* only two. Maeve is six.'

'I wonder is it normal for a six-year-old to want a doll's house anyway,' said my mother. So they had another hour looking up Normal-Six-Year-Olds in Dr Spock or its equivalent, decided it was boringly normal and inconvenient, and went back to work.

They got bricks and stones in from the garden. They looked up a book called *One Thousand Things a Boy Can Do,* but none of them included making a doll's house. My father became interested in one of the things

166

a boy could do which was digging a tunnel in the garden to irrigate the flower beds.

'That's all we need on Christmas Day,' said my mother wearily, 'for the neighbours to see you irrigating the flower beds with tunnels.'

It was nearly dawn. The fat cherub was asleep with no idea of anything being amiss. They came into my room, set up the blackboard, and wrote a note on it with one of the pieces of chalk!

'Dear Maeve, Your chimney is too narrow and I can't get the doll's house down it. Please do not be upset. It will arrive as an extra gift sometime in January. You have been a good girl. All the reindeer are asking for you. Love from Santa Clause.'

It was morning and with shining eyes I was beating on them, begging them to wake up. After only two hours' sleep this wasn't easy for them to do. They showed great alarm. Was I going to threaten to leave home! Were there tears and tantrums which would spoil the day for everyone. Not at all.

'You'll never believe it,' I said. 'Santa Clause wrote me a note. In his own writing. It's on an old blackboard or something, but it's obviously very valuable. Nobody has seen Santa Claus's writing before. We'll have to show it to everyone. We might lend it to a museum.'

It was a good Christmas, like all our Christmases were together; the only thing that makes me sad at this time of year is that I may have forgotten to tell them that. . . but perhaps they knew.

My First Book, 1976

167

THE CHRISTMAS PANTOMIME

John Ryan

Nothing revives so many good memories of childhood as the word 'pantomime'. Nothing evokes so well the magic of long ago, the spirit of Christmas past.

Time passes and it becomes harder to recall what a child really feels about the season (as against what we think it should feel), just as it becomes increasingly more difficult to see properly through the layers of irrelevancies and gift wrappings that mask what should be at the heart of Christmas.

Pantomime for some reason has retained the authentic flavour of the time. Perhaps it is because the people who give us this yearly confection are wise enough not to tamper with the cooking of it too much and offer it to us as the traditional fare that it is.

Dublin could once boast of about a half dozen of these entertainments each year, with the major productions at the Gaiety and Olympia theatres. True, the mammoth Theatre Royal also attempted to give us something in the same vein, but pantomime however well presented fell flat on its face in that vast neo-Aztec jazz-modern mausoleum of the varieties.

The Gaiety held the slight edge over the Olympia as far as elegance was concerned, catering as it did for the Rathmines and Rathgar and Foxrock carriage trade. I can still hear the Minervas and Delages purring alongside its canopied vestibule and see invaluable cargoes of silk and satin-bedecked pig-tailed moppets being discharged. These argosies were later to be observed consuming vast quantities of chocolates, framed in the red plush and gilt of the dress circle boxes like bevies of diminutive Czarinas.

But the Olympia had its own special attractions too. It was more spicy and less cloying and it was raffish by nature. It was the temple of Vaudeville and Edwardian beyond words. The patrons expected and got a heady measure of uninhibited jokes and business as well as splendidly high-kicking 'gals'. It was only when men who balanced billard cues on their noses took to the stage that a considerable number of the audience took to the bars. But to us, concerned only with the story of Little Red Riding Hood or Puss-In-Boots, as it was being tenuously unwound, all these happenings were grossly superfluous.

There was a carpeted hush and a lingering aroma of coffee about the Gaiety that not so much screamed as whispered wealth, so that the discreet bar there played but a minor role in the larger Palm Court setting. On the other hand the Olympia's was a superb rococo saloon that echoed to full-blooded ribaldry both during the intervals and, as we

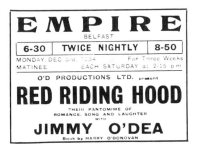

have noted, those periods during the show which the customers
deemed to be *longeurs*.

The lord of these revels for more than thirty years was Jimmy O'Dea.
He must have been one of the greatest Dames in the long history of
pantomime. He was often partnered by that most gifted of comediennes
Maureen Potter who in time became his most worthy successor at the
Gaiety. No memory of the art will be even partly complete without him.

Let us bring back the scene: at long last the house lights dim and the
compulsive chatter ceases, to be replaced by the frou-frou of tafetta and
the rustle of sweet-wrappers. The footlights suffuse the velvet curtains
in amber and gold and the orchestra attacks the overture with vigour. At
last the tab goes up to reveal a village square all ablaze with light as the
limes and travelling spots find their targets. It is somewhere in
Ruritania. The lads and lassies of this place are chirping animatedly each
to each, having been assembled here for some reason of which we will
learn more anon.

They are in fact *all* girls, as is, indeed, the principal boy who now trips
onstage to the cheers of the villagers, in shiny tights and high-heeled
shoes. I once found myself trying to explain this and the fact that the
Dame was a man but the Good Fairy a woman to a friend but he
mumbled something about it seeming to be 'incredibly bent', so I
thought the better of it and dropped the subject. The conversation took
place in Hoboken, New Jersey, where they never heard of pantomime.

Then the principal girl and the Baron and his shady assistants come
forward and introduce themselves with all the formal ritual of oriental
drama. Indeed pantomime may be the nearest thing we have to
Japanese *Noh* drama. All this is but a build-up for the great moment
when the conductor responding to some unseen cue (or was it that little
red light that went on for a moment?) suddenly rushes the orchestra
through the last bars of 'Biddy Mulligan the Pride of the Coombe'
whereupon our hero bursts on to the stage either on a bike, in a car,
astride a donkey, by balloon or the simpler and even more popular
expedient of sliding through on his derrière.

And from that moment on, we were Jimmy O'Dea's children and
Christmas had been, once more, marvellously accomplished.

Sunday Miscellancy, 1975

CHRISTMAS SHOPPING

Louis MacNeice

Spending beyond their income on gifts for Christmas –
Swing doors and crowded lifts and draperied jungles –
What shall we buy for our husbands and sons
    Different from last year?

Foxes hang by their noses behind plate glass –
Scream of macaws across festoons of paper –
Only the faces on the boxes of chocolates are free
    From boredom and crowsfeet.

Sometimes a chocolate-box girl escapes in the flesh,
Lightly manoeuvres the crowd, trilling with laughter;
After a couple of years her feet and her brain will
    Tire like the others.

The great windows marshal their troops for assault on the purse
Something-and-eleven the yard, hoodwinking logic,
The eleventh hour draining the gurgling pennies
    Down to the conduits

Down to the sewers of money – rats and marshgas –
Bubbling in maundering music under the pavement;
Here go the hours of routine, the weight on our eyelids –
    Pennies on corpses'.

While over the street in the centrally heated public
Library dwindling figures with sloping shoulders
And hands in pockets, weighted in the boots like chessmen,
    Stare at the printed

Columns of ads, the quickset road to riches,
Starting at a little and temporary but once we're
Started who knows whether we shan't continue,
    Salaries rising,

Rising like a salmon against the bullnecked river,
Bound for the spawning-ground of care-free days –
Good for a fling before the golden wheels run
    Down to a standstill.

And Christ is born – The nursery glad with baubles,
Alive with light and washable paint and children's
Eyes, expects as its due the accidental
Loot of a system.

Smell of the South – oranges in silver paper,
Dates and ginger, the benison of firelight,
The blue flames dancing round the brandied raisins,
Smiles from above them,

Hands from above them as of gods but really
These their parents, always seen from below, them-
Selves are always anxious looking across the
Fence to the future –

Out there lies the future gathering quickly
Its blank momentum; through the tubes of London
The dead winds blow the crowds like beasts in flight from
Fire in the forest.

The little firtrees palpitate with candles
In hundreds of chattering households where the suburb
Straggles like nervous handwriting, the margin
Blotted with smokestacks.

Further out on the coast the lighthouse moves its
Arms of light through the fog that wads our welfare,
Moves its arms like a giant at Swedish drill whose
Mind is a vacuum.

Collected Poems, 1966

Wud yez tread on the tail of me coat?

CHRISTMAS IN CALLAN, CO. KILKENNY, 1828

Humphrey O'Sullivan

24th. . . Wednesday. Christmas Eve, a fast day. A thin-clouded morning. A mild south west wind. A blue-skied day, as fine as May-day. The poor people are buying pork chops, pigs' heads, soggy beef, big joints of old sows' loins, and small bits of old rams, as all the good meat has been already bought up by the well-off, well-fed people. He who comes last will be the loser, as usual. . .

25th. . . Christmas Day. Before daybreak the moon was shining in a clear sky without cloud or mist, welcoming the good Infant Jesus. A big drum being beaten at five o'clock. Fifes and clarinets being played by the youth of the town.

26th. . . St Stephen's Day. It is difficult to go hunting with a pack of hounds today, for it is extremely hard for the hunters to follow them, the country is so wet. Snow on *Sliabh na mBan Fionn* from the bottom to the top of *Suí Finn*, that is, the peak of *Sliabh na mBan*.

The town rabble going from door to door with a wren in a holly bush, asking for money so that they can be drunk tonight. It is a bad habit to give it to them. Few people at Mass in Callan today because of the wet morning. It was very different three years ago today, when fourteen people were killed at the Brothers' Chapel, and a hundred injured. It was a dreadful affair.

The Diary of Humphrey O'Sullivan
(translated by Tomás de Bhaldraithe, 1979)

THE SPIRIT OF CHRISTMAS

Eamon Kelly

When we were bigger we were let go to midnight Mass in the Friary. Two Third Order men at the door. Very officious, sniffing in case anyone got in with a sign of drink on him. Christmas Day'd be quiet. There'd be a goose for the dinner, or a cock. There was post that time on Christmas Day and every house the postman'd go into, especially if he had a letter from America, he'd have to take a nip. At the end of his round the poor man'd be stocious. What harm was that. He'd be sober and correct for the rest of the year!

Once you got into long trousers and had a few bob in your pocket, what you looked forward to was Stephen's Night. All'd hit for the village. A big night of dancing. Even before the returned Yanks built the dance halls there'd be dancing in the kitchen of the public house. 'Twas Ned Connor that'd be on the concertina and he was a gifted player, but like many musicians he liked the drop. Ned was noted. The wife warned him one Christmas Eve to be sure and go to confession. Ned forgot all about it until he was passing the Friary on the way home good and full, and seeing the goldy cross on the gate out of the corner of his eye, he was reminded of it and he went in.

Sliding along the seat as those before him moved towards the confessional, he finally got to the box and went in. It can be stuffy enough inside there when old people are in and out, and whoever was at the other side had a long story to tell, so that the fumes of the drink rising in Ned's head made him drowsy and he nodded off. When the shutter came across with a bang, he woke up, and said;

'The same again and turn on the light in the snug!'

That Christmas night the wife's aunt, Auntie Pegg, was visiting 'em, a fierce druidess of a one, and she wasn't long in pointing out to Ned the error of his ways. She made him go down on his knees and promise he'd give up the drink, the ruination of body and soul! So he went into the Mercy Convent and took the pledge from Sister Benedict. And to every-

173

one's surprise kept it – well, until one day he met some old comrades in town. He didn't want to go into the public house but they said it would only be the *one*. He came out of the place legless, he was so bad when he got into his own house he had to hold on to the back of the chair to maintain any relationship with the perpendicular.

His wife's aunt came down the stairs in her night attire, and standing on the bottom step, her hand on the newel post, she read him a lesson:

'A nice state to be in after the promise he gave to his wife and to his children and to myself and to the Man above! And look at the *geatch* of him now,' she said. 'Look at him now, his face puffed and bloated! His soul as black as porter! And what would you do,' she said to him, 'if the Lord called on you this minute?'

'To tell you the truth, auntie,' he said, 'I couldn't stir a leg!'

The Rub of a Relic, 1978

from WREATHS

Michael Longley

The Greengrocer

He ran a good shop, and he died
Serving even the death-dealers
Who found him busy as usual
Behind the counter, organised
With holly wreaths for Christmas,
Fir trees on the pavement outside.

Astrologers or three wise men
Who may shortly be setting out
For a small house up the Shankill
Or the Falls, should pause on their way
To buy gifts at Jim Gibson's shop,
Dates and chestnuts and tangerines.

Poems 1963–1983, 1985

I FOLLOW A STAR

Joseph Campbell

I follow a star
Burning deep in the blue
A sign on the hills
Lit for me and for you.

Moon-red is the star,
Halo-ringed like a rood,
Christ's heart in its heart set,
Streaming with blood.

Follow the gilly
Beyond to the west:
He leads where Christ lies
On Mary's white breast.

King, priest, prophet –
A child, and no more –
Adonai the Maker!
Come, let us adore.

The Irish Christmas, 1918

THE CRIB

Susan Mitchell

Day closes in the cabin dim,
They light the Christmas candle tall
For Him who is the light of all.
They deck the little crib for Him
Whose cradle is earth's swinging ball.

The Irish Christmas, 1918

THE BOXING DAY SHOOT

Sam Hanna Bell

Every Boxing Day the men of our family met to shoot over a small farm in County Down. It being a custom they came without invitation. About fifteen men gathered at the house with nine guns between them including the two farm guns. I'm sure about the number of guns for I was at that age when a strange gun was of more interest than a stranger.

On Christmas Eve a sudden and bitter frost had grasped the countryside, and the following morning its whitened knuckles shone off roofs and trees and rocks. The air was as clear and plangent as crystal glass so that a bark or a shot rang over the fields and echoed through the hills like receding footsteps. In the house the kitchen range roared and blew until its rings and orifices glowed poppy-red and scalding water had to be drawn from the brass tap in its hinch. Outside in the close the frozen earth had curled up between the cobbles leaving them sunken in their pits like sightless eyes. I was unable to draw water from the well, and when the man of the house came with a spade to break the ice, diamonds glittered in his beard.

But overnight the weather softened and a raw white mist rose out of the small lough three fields away and crept into the hedges and the alders and reeds that fringed the water. As we set out the sky was not so much calm as dead. Everything was motionless and the only sounds were our voices and the susurration of our feet through the dripping grass. A shallow burn, the Longstone, wandered down from the drumlins and ran along the bottom of the field on its way to the lough. We scrambled across the narrow coffin-shaped stone that gave the burn its name. Several men who had straggled away to the left were leaping the burn, their emptied guns held over their heads. This sodden rush-covered waste bordering the lough was traditionally the turning-point of the shooting party, and on this dreich morning no one felt inclined to go further. The *convention* had been fulfilled for another year, two or three shots had been fired, and as everybody agreed, this had ceased to be a good countryside for sport.

'I think,' said the son of the house, 'we'll turn. The dinner'll be waiting.' There was a murmur of agreement, without betraying, of course, any sign of eagerness.

'We had bad luck today,' said the young man.

'Not a word,' cried several of the visitors, 'sure the district's shot out, and that's a fact!'

In sharp contradiction we heard three shots fired down by the lough. The fusillade startled everyone. Some of the men ran off through the rushes and dank bracken until they had a clear view of the lough. There they stopped abruptly, shouting and gesticulating. I ran after them and by clambering on a fallen alder I could see the surface of the water. A swan was milling round and round in the centre of the lough beating one great wing.

'Look!' shouted a man and pointed. Two figures were clambering up a distant field. 'Who are they?' someone asked.

The man narrowed his eyes to assist his memory rather than his sight. 'Those two young fellows from Belfast – Hughie McVeigh's nephews.' The swan, raising its wing with great effort, was drifting towards the opposite shore. The men around me were murmuring '. . . belong to the King. . . unlawful to shoot. . . royal. . . birds. . .'

A man plucked off his hat and flung it savagely to the ground. 'The dirty whelps!' he shouted. The young man, with all the threads of involved and intricate relationships to keep disentangled, held up a deprecating hand. 'Now, now,' he said, 'now, now. . .'

A big fellow, a neighbour of ours, threw open the breech of his gun and fumbled in his jacket pocket. 'I'll finish her off,' he said. He strode away through the rushes to the little jetty of corrugated iron from where in the summer the local lads floated out frogs with hooks in their bellies to catch pike.

The corrugated sheet dipped under his weight and sent a tremor through the melting water-thin ice. I saw the big man raise his gun and straddle himself steady as the bird floundered into his sights. It took the blast of hail in the hollow between wing and body. A spout of feathers flew up, paused, and idled down to the surface of the reddened water.

That was the last time the men of the family gathered for the Boxing Day shoot. Looking back now, I suspect that the custom had lost its spontaneity many years before. Feathered out by the ritual of hospitality it floated, charming but inanimate, on the surface of sentiment. It only required the unwitting brutality of two city lads to blow it to fragments.

The Boxing Day shoot persisted in many parts of Ulster, for a custom is myriad-headed and cannot be finished at a thrust; but on that Boxing Day it died on one farm and in time the news of its death idled across a district.

Hello, Big Lad, 1977

ACKNOWLEDGEMENTS

Grateful acknowledgement is made to:

Appletree Press Ltd for permission to reprint 'The Boxing Day Shoot' by Sam Hanna Bell from *Hello Big Lad* (ed. Neill Speers) and 'The Poor Little Clerk Who'd Never Got a Christmas Card Before' by Paul Yates from *Sky Made of Stone*;

Harry Barton for permission to quote from *Yours Again, Mr Mooney*;

Roland Benner for permission to reprint 'Christmas Wayfarers' and 'Saint Bride's Lullaby at Bethlehem' by Cathal O'Byrne;

Simon Campbell and Allen Figgis & Co. for permission to reprint 'I Follow a Star' by Joseph Campbell;

Lucy Rodgers Cohen for permission to reprint 'White Christmas' by W.R. Rodgers, © W.R. Rodgers 1941;

Curtis Brown Ltd for permission to reprint 'The Nativity' by C.S. Lewis;

J.M. Dent and Sons Ltd for permission to reprint 'Christmas Eve' by Ruth and Celia Duffin from *Escape,* and a wood engraving from *Coming Down the Wye* by Robert Gibbings;

André Deutsch Ltd for permission to quote from *The Emperor of Ice Cream* by Brian Moore;

Dolmen Press Ltd for permission to reprint 'A Christmas Card' from *The Dead Kingdom,* 'Christmas Morning' from *The Rough Field* and 'The Mummer Speaks' from *Poisoned Lands,* all by John Montague;

Dublin Historical Record for permission to reprint 'Christmas in Old Dublin' by Annie P. Smithson;

Duckworth & Co. Ltd for permission to reprint 'The Christmas Rhymers' from *An Ulster Childhood* and to quote from 'Turkey and Ham' from *The Ballygullion Bus,* both by Lynn Doyle;

Dundalgan Press Ltd for permission to quote from *At Slieve Gullion's Foot* by Michael J. Murphy;

Faber and Faber Ltd for permission to reprint 'The Last Mummer' from *Wintering Out* by Seamus Heaney, and 'Christmas Shopping' by Louis MacNeice;

John Farquharson Ltd for permission to quote from 'Oweneen the Sprat' by E. OE. Somerville & Martin Ross;

Rowel Friers for permission to reprint cartoons;

J. Anthony Gaughan for permission to quote from *Memoirs of Constable Jeremiah Mee, RIC*;

The Estate of Robert Gibbings for permission to reproduce wood engravings by Robert Gibbings;

Goldsmith Press Ltd for permission to quote from *The Complete Poems of Patrick Kavanagh,* published by The Goldsmith Press, Newbridge, Co. Kildare;

Hamish Hamilton Ltd for permission to quote from *The Christmas Tree* by Jennifer Johnston;

John Hewitt for permission to reprint 'The Carol Singers';

Hutchinson Ltd for permission to quote from *Borstal Boy* by Brendan Behan;

Irish Academic Press for permission to quote from *The Religious Songs of Connacht* by Douglas Hyde;

The Irish Times Ltd for permission to quote from *Man Bites Dog* by Donal Foley and from *My First Book* by Maeve Binchy;

Brendan Kennelly and Allen Figgis & Co for permission to reprint 'The Wren-boy' and 'A Kerry Christmas' by Brendan Kennelly;

Benedict Kiely for permission to quote from *Land Without Stars*;

Michael Longley, Salamander Press and Gallery Press for permission to quote from 'Wreaths' from *Poems 1963–1983*;

Mercier Press Ltd for permission to quote from *The Rub of a Relic* by Eamon Kelly and from *The Diary of Humphrey O'Sullivan*, translated by Tomás de Bhaldraithe;

O'Brien Press Ltd for permission to quote from *Jimeen* by Padraig Ó Siochfhradha, translated by Patricia Egan, Peter Fallon and Ide Ni Laoghaire, and from *Gur Cake and Coal Blocks* by Eamon Mac Thomais;

Frank Ormsby for permission to reprint 'In Lieu of Carols' from *A Store of Candles*;

Oxford University Press Ltd for permission to quote from *The Irish Journal of Elizabeth Smith* (ed. David Thomson), and from *The Islandman* by Tomás O'Crohan (translated by Robin Flower 1951);

A.D. Peters & Co. Ltd for permission to quote from *Leinster, Munster and Connaught* by Frank O'Connor © 1950, and from *The Stories of Frank O'Connor*;

Poolbeg Press for permission to quote from *Collected Short Stories of Michael McLaverty*;

John Ryan for permission to reprint 'The Christmas Pantomime';

James Simmons for permission to reprint 'Seasonal Greeting' and 'Nativity';

A.J. Smyth for permission to quote from *Souls of Poor Folk* by Alexander Irvine;

The Society of Authors for permission to quote from the works of George Bernard Shaw;

The Society of Authors as the literary representative of the Estate of James Joyce for permission to quote from 'The Dead' from *Dubliners* and from *Portrait of the Artist as a Young Man*, both by James Joyce;

Talbot Press Ltd for permission to quote from *Peig* by Peig Sayers (translated into English by Bryan MacMahon); and for permission to reprint 'Christmas Parties and Paper Hats' from *My Hat Blew Off* and 'The Carol-singers' from *Funnily Enough*, both by J.D. Sheridan;

Joseph Tomelty for permission to reproduce 'McCooey's Christmas Party';

Ulster Journal of Archaeology for permission to quote from 'An Account of a Journey of Captain Josias Bodley in the Year 1602';

Ward River Press for permission to quote from *Sam McAughtry's Belfast*;

Anne Yeats and Michael B. Yeats, owners of the copyright of Jack B. Yeats, for permission to reproduce Christmas cards originally published by the Cuala Press;

Michael B. Yeats and Macmillan London Ltd for permission to reprint 'The Magi' and to quote from 'Upon a Dying Lady' by W.B. Yeats.

INDEX OF AUTHORS

A 85 88 4
854 68